Mastering Boundary Setting

Establishing Boundaries for Personal Growth and Happiness

Eden Storm

Table of Contents

Introduction

The more you value yourself, the healthier your boundaries are. –Lorraine Nilon

I'll be upfront with you. When I first read the quotation above, the first thing that raced to mind was, *Sure, easier said than done, friend!* I remember that at the time it just felt like such a stretch, but the quotation lingered and forced me to wonder. My initial plan wasn't to construct boundaries; the truth is, people always spoke about their presence and whatnot, but I always thought it was hocus-pocus or something. The thing that stuck with me was whether or not I valued myself. I know, such a loaded wonder, right? But think about it; if we sincerely valued ourselves, we wouldn't allow ourselves to creep into negative spaces, right? If the establishment of a boundary can prohibit negative spaces, then surely, based on the value we have for ourselves, we'd have established boundaries.

To me, boundaries always felt like something you constructed because you had no backbone—I know, rather harsh, right? But then I reached a point in my life where I could barely hold my feet on the ground, and it felt as if each time I drew breath, I was trying to catch up on breathing because things were constantly moving without consideration for my mind. But I've always known that life has this annoying habit of getting busy quickly, warping you into a sort of riptide where the only thing to do is hold on tight and hope that you make it through to the end of the week or, if you're like me, the end of the month. The truth is, I knew that I needed to change. Effective, healthy boundaries offer so many wonderful benefits to your well-being:

- By enforcing boundaries, you'll discover how powerful you are—I mean it. Before the introduction of boundaries in my life, comparing myself to power felt ridiculous. But boundaries require patience and strength; they're difficult to uphold and constantly being fought at by others who simply can't comprehend your need for them. Power is there, though; if anything, it's taught me to trust myself.

- Boundaries can affect your perspective on resentment and ultimately transform your relationships. I think that we're so often drawn to one state of mind that we forget to take a step back and reconsider everything before crafting an opinion.

- Your self-esteem is going to get a boost. Before boundaries, I was the kind of person who avoided the mirror, not due to insecurity, but because I felt embarrassed about the kind of person I was: The kind that didn't stand up for myself, didn't reach for opportunity, and always gave up too quickly. My low self-esteem tormented me. But when I introduced boundaries, I began to effectively rebuild myself with self-care and this helped me find my true potential, and by potential, I mean helping redefine success and capability for myself.

- You're going to learn how to identify your triggers; this is great for you. In the beginning, I often found myself in stressful situations and would lay awake at night wondering how I got where I got, and it made me miserable. Also, this only worsened my self-esteem. But when we're able to know what harms our mental health, we're able to avoid those situations with mindfulness. By "avoidance," I mean it in the healthy sense of the word—to avoid, we must first acknowledge.

- You're going to get to know yourself properly. I think that when we're not intentional about our time, the self becomes unfamiliar. The issue with this is that if the self is unfamiliar, it is impressionable, and society has a way of forcing its narrative on it. We often find ourselves overly focused on superficial news that offers us no care for our mental health. But through effective boundaries and with self-care you're going to learn to understand yourself and your emotions.

It's a journey, and it's difficult. Despite how intrusive boundaries are to our identity, they affect those around us too. I'll be honest, some relationships couldn't withstand change. However, here I am; I'm doing better, and I still have the comfort of trusted friends and family. My point is that things are likely going to seem as if they're going downhill for you, but they're not going that far down. Things are going to pick up again. I wrote this book to help you. I know how superficial that might sound. But it's the truth. I mentioned that I struggled with low self-esteem and often found myself in stressful situations that dangerously overwhelmed me. I feared for my mental health. I was afraid that I would suffer intense burnout and lose everything I had.

It's not that I had much, but I worked incredibly hard for it, and maybe you know what that's like. Maybe you're in the same situation and struggling to make it through a difficult time, or whenever you manage to make it through, you find yourself struggling to change the circumstances that forced you into this position. I wrote this book to help you understand yourself a bit better. In the list of things I mentioned, we'll cover those topics alongside many others. We'll learn about habits and why they should never be broken but merely converted into healthy ones. We'll chat about change and why, whenever a boundary is evoked, people push up against us. You'll learn about self-care, the numerous benefits it garners, and how it brilliantly pairs with boundaries.

However, more importantly, we will also discuss the presence of joy in our lives. Society has the habit of displaying only the pretty side of getting your life in order, and though the overall process is pretty, it will promote personal growth. The process is uncomfortable and difficult to practice. Sometimes we lose sight of important things, and this is okay. And we'll discuss joy. Joy is an essence lodged within our well-being; self-care activates this emotion. But I think I've said enough for now; let's begin.

Chapter 1:

Understanding Boundaries

And that is how change happens. One gesture. One person. One moment at a time. –Libba Bray

According to the Merriam-Webster dictionary, a boundary is "Something that indicates or fixes a limit or extent" (Merriam Webster 2024, para. 1). However, for some of us, the simplest definition is that a boundary is a line that mustn't be crossed by anyone, especially ourselves. Boundaries are like those Russian nesting dolls, and as each doll fits into the other, they ideally protect each other. Is this not the point of a boundary—to protect? Most people confuse the diversity of a boundary—for example, think of those nesting dolls. A boundary isn't one thing or form; there are several of them that occur throughout our lives and within our lifestyle choices. Remember that the key to the lasting success of a boundary is its health. Most people misunderstand the personal urgency of establishing boundaries and assume that a well-set boundary preserves positivity, success, or happiness. This is somewhat true; a good set of boundaries can ultimately lead to a better and healthier life.

What Are Personal Boundaries?

Personal boundaries are described as a set of life skills, guidelines, rules, or limits (your choice) found within each person; this means that a boundary is first and foremost associated with the self before it is with the exterior world. Personal boundaries are considered more mundane; they establish our preferences or likes and dislikes. For example, maybe you don't like hugging, so you establish this as a dislike, which is a boundary. Think of your boundaries as your daily preferences that get you through each day.

What Are the Benefits of Setting Boundaries?

1. It's going to promote autonomy.

2. It's going to prevent burnout and decrease your stress levels.

3. It's going to help you develop self-respect which will ultimately demand respect from others.

4. It's going to improve your emotional health.

5. It's going to improve your relationships.

6. Your self-care abilities are going to improve.

7. You're going to feel a lot more comfortable with yourself.

8. It's going to improve your self-esteem which will affect your levels of confidence and compassion toward yourself and others.

9. You're going to be able to understand yourself better, which will allow those around you to understand what you need and want.

Can Boundaries Be Paired with Self-Care?

Yes, (and we'll get into self-care in a few chapters), but many people don't know that boundaries are just another word or form of self-care. Now, I know that you've heard about self-care before, right? Socially, it's about prioritizing a series of practices, like beauty, mindfulness, diet, etc., to better oneself. The type of self-care I'm referring to defines the practice as a collection of actions an individual tries to maintain to prevent poor health (in its broad sense) and preserve their well-being (mentally, spiritually, physically, and emotionally). Also, self-care is an essential skill that each person should acquire to generate success. I think that for many, the idea of self-care is about creating comfort, and though I'm all about comfort, I can't disregard how uncomfortable life is—you know that basic saying, right? To make it through life, you must get comfortable with the uncomfortable. This is extremely true, especially regarding modernity.

The consistency of change—brought on by consumer culture and technological advancement—keeps us busy. Honestly, do you feel that there are factions in your life that constantly overlap each other? For example, with some people, a no is a no, but with others, a no eventually becomes a yes. This was a regularity in my life, and all it did was cause me misery. Most of the time, it felt as if I was always doing double the work on a daily (and emotional) level, sabotaging the potential for success. Looking back on things now, it's not so much that I felt sorry for myself, *but I did.* I just wish someone had come up to me sooner and informed me about the power of setting boundaries and about the belief in a self-care practice. But here's the thing though, to succeed at self-care, you must establish your boundaries.

I'll admit that the interconnectivity of boundaries and self-care, change, and habits is a bit strange—it's the full picture, though. I think that my mistake leading up to creating healthy and successful boundaries was that I couldn't see or envision the full picture. Due to the rush of modernism, we are fed incomplete information about life, and this is why so many of us feel sabotaged by the choices we make. My head is running to the hype of morning and evening routines. I remember thinking a series of curious things about the people— particularly the ones following a 30-step preparation process— and failing to realize that those were boundaries being evoked. I'm not suggesting that we all grab pen and paper and begin jotting down 30-step processes (if it's for you, go for it). I suppose I'm saying that if you're like me (failing to notice that a boundary was being evoked), then you don't see the full picture either.

This is okay—and no, I'm not patronizing you, just letting you know that this is the overall point of the book. We're here to strengthen our relationship with self-care and we're going to use boundaries as a means of succeeding. Remember, I said that a self-care practice is a collection of actions—so, think of these actions as your boundaries, and without them, every positive thing you do withers away into non-essentialism. I compared boundaries to a Russian nesting doll. The first reason was to express the idea of barriers and how enforcing healthy boundaries can prohibit negative experiences. The second reason is that each boundary possesses its own set of rules that allow them to perfectly merge and respect each other—respect is the golden rule.

Why Do I Need Boundaries?

There are various reasons, and yet the simplest reason is because you're currently struggling in life. Remember that boundaries are a set of realistic limitations that we impose on ourselves—the boundary is about us, about what we deem acceptable and tolerable. A common misinterpretation about setting boundaries is that trauma or low self-esteem must be present, but this isn't true. Each of us needs boundaries in our lives. I've listed ten examples of why you might need to set boundaries in your life.

WHY YOU MAY NEED BOUNDARIES	
The Reason	**The Boundary**
Saying "no" is an issue for you. This is a common issue for many people; we tend to find ourselves in situations where it's easier to agree and approve, as opposed to saying "no" due to fear of disappointing them, being called selfish, or because you're a people-pleaser.	The solution to this issue is simple, all you have to do is use "no" more confidently. Here are some examples: 1. Use "no" as a complete sentence: "No, thank you; I won't be able to." 2. Don't make it personal: "Thank you for thinking about me, but I won't be able to help you." 3. Be vague and firm: "Thank you for considering me, but this isn't going to work for me." 4. Use a referral: "Thank you for considering me, but I won't be able

WHY YOU MAY NEED BOUNDARIES

The Reason	The Boundary
	to help you; why don't you ask Paul?"
	5. The last-minute boundary: "Unfortunately, I'm fully booked for the month and won't be able to go with you."
	6. Be gracious: "I'm touched that you asked, but my time is fully committed elsewhere."
	7. Time to consider: "Let me think about it and I'll get back to you."
	8. Respect yourself: "No, but here is what I can do instead..."
	9. Specify when: "None of those dates work for me, but I'd love to meet up with you; send me some more dates." or "I'm unavailable until February; could we meet up to discuss dates closer to that time?"
	10. Show gratitude: "I appreciate that you thought of me and all your support, but I'm sorry that I won't be able to help you out this time."

WHY YOU MAY NEED BOUNDARIES

The Reason	The Boundary
You're always overwhelmed with tasks and have constructed the narrative that you're fully capable of getting it all done. You might even portray this narrative to people and feel you're *expected* to do it all, which is also why you have issues with saying "no." In fact, there are common areas where feelings of being overwhelmed are experienced within the workplace environment.	The solution to dealing with overrun emotions is to refocus and set reasonable limitations with people; here are some examples: 1. Incorporate the usage of saying "no" when your emotions are too heavy. 2. Leave situations and experiences that rile up your emotions. 3. Be upfront with your limitations— for example, if you're only staying for an hour, be clear. 4. Always check in with your feelings; if things feel off or too much, leave and find someplace quiet. Practice mindful breathing while reflecting on your emotions. 5. Let go of the idea of fixing or solving other people's difficulties. Being a supportive friend and actively listening is enough. 6. Clarify your personal space for those around you, and if it's triggered, leave the environment. This is particularly important in

WHY YOU MAY NEED BOUNDARIES

The Reason	The Boundary
	workplace environments.
	7. Be honest about the number of projects you can take on.
You're apologizing for everything and nothing. This one is almost habitual; it's basically muscle memory. In fact, for many, this is a defensive mechanism and stems from the household culture we grew up in. The damaging issue with always apologizing is that it cultivates self-doubt, affects your self-esteem, and affects your mental health.	The solution to this issue requires a bit of practice. Here's what to do: 1. First, work on understanding your triggers; since they may vary between person and environment, they could be: • Questions about your character. • Your morals. • Conflict within your friendship, etc. 2. When a trigger arises, take a moment to pause and reflect before you habitually begin apologizing. This will require practice to perfect; you're naturally inclined to apologize, so it's going to rewire the brain. Be kind to yourself during this time and remember that self-awareness counts.

WHY YOU MAY NEED BOUNDARIES	
The Reason	**The Boundary**
	(We'll discuss the benefits of change and habits in the next chapter.)
	3. Because apologies are automated, a simple approach is to rephrase the apology. For example, instead of saying, "I'm sorry that I'm late or for making you wait," You could say, "Thank you for being patient; I appreciate it."
	4. Practice being more assertive. The best place to start is by using "I" at the start of the sentence; this solidifies yourself and the emotion within the situation. Being assertive is about being comfortable enough to have an opinion and share it with those around you without feeling guilt or judgment.
	Another great way of solidifying your relationship with assertiveness is with self-affirmations. For example, each morning, check in with yourself and start with something like, "I am worthy and capable of completing my goals for today."
You tend to stoop to other	Here are suitable solutions to help you: 1. Don't take it personally; most of

WHY YOU MAY NEED BOUNDARIES

The Reason	The Boundary
people's level when things aren't working out, and usually this occurs because it's easier to go along with the flow of things despite your discomfort, as opposed to removing yourself from the situation or changing the subjectivity of the situation. Another reason we stoop to others' level is because we feel as if we're not being heard by those around us.	the time, the issue directed at you has nothing to do with you. 2. If you have an issue with someone, it is okay to politely talk to them about it. There is absolutely nothing wrong with letting someone know how they made you feel or that they crossed a boundary. 3. Mind your body language; when we become angry, upset, or irritated, the body will tense up. Sometimes, to the other person, this will present an unapproachable demeanor. 4. Always ask for clarification; language can be confusing and, most of the time, misinterpreted. If something is directed at you, simply ask them to clarify themselves.
You're constantly complaining about certain people, and it's beginning to take a toll on your	The best solution is to change our attitude regarding the situation arising. Here are some practical tips to follow: 1. Accept the challenge; the truth is, people can't be changed, or rather,

WHY YOU MAY NEED BOUNDARIES

The Reason	The Boundary
mental health and has even started to negatively affect those around you. When we're drawn into the mode of complaining about situations and people, there is a clear need for the establishment of boundaries.	you can't change them. The best thing to do is accept that whatever it is, it can't be changed by you, but must simply be accepted. 2. Allowing yourself the comfort to vent every now and then and keeping our emotions on the inside is unhealthy and only leads us toward a breaking point. Know that it's okay to vent, but don't attach to them. 3. Be aware of your mindset; a great way to change your mind is by applying assertiveness to your behavior (see apologizing section). 4. Accept responsibility for your role in the situation. Even though your reasons for complaining are legitimate, complaining is a passive activity that is not healthy or beneficial to your success. 5. Stop labeling everything, and remember that when we're complaining, it's because we're judging a person or the situation. So, remember to pause before responding.

WHY YOU MAY NEED BOUNDARIES

The Reason	The Boundary
You often feel powerless, and this feeling varies throughout various aspects of your life, for example with your career, relationships, health choices, or financial choices. When you feel powerless, it means that you have no control over your life, and this sensation arises for many reasons, like feeling stressed, constantly defeated by an experience, or simply feeling as if we're no longer being heard.	The solution to this issue requires you to be more constructive toward your challenges. Here are some tips: 1. Work on a routine; this might seem boring or even unrealistic, but by following a specific routine each day, you're able to develop new and healthier habits. 2. Focus on what's going well; now, this doesn't mean ignoring the bad or your difficulties, only that you pay attention to the good things more. 3. Go slow, don't overwhelm yourself with change (especially regarding the creation of boundaries), and take your time at the start. It might feel as if nothing's successfully happening, but believe me, the more progress you make, the more consistent your newer habits will become. 4. Work on your fitness goal. You may not consider yourself a physically active person, but by boosting your physical attributes, you're going to improve your

WHY YOU MAY NEED BOUNDARIES

The Reason	The Boundary
	physical and mental health and boost your overall mood, which will effectively help you create boundaries.
You often lose your temper and feel close to seriously raging at those around you. This usually occurs because you're feeling irritable due to inward stress. When we don't have proper boundaries established with people, we allow certain traits or difficulties to gnaw at us inwardly, and often this anger and frustration get misdirected.	This one is slightly trickier, but the solutions to this issue are straightforward. Here's what to do: 1. Always think before you speak; it's so easy to say something worth regretting after the fact. Take a few minutes, breathe, and gather your thoughts. 2. When calm, begin to express your concerns. Use direct and clear language. 3. Recognize your triggers and try to stay clear of them. It's always recommended to walk away and find a safe space to calm down. 4. Stop holding grudges; it's not going to get you anywhere and will help you do away with negative feelings. Letting go doesn't mean dismissing the behavior of the person, but simply not allowing anger and tension to linger.

WHY YOU MAY NEED BOUNDARIES	
The Reason	**The Boundary**
	5. Work on exploring possible relaxation mechanisms to help you deal with your anger. Walking away and breathing are good steps.
Sometimes you blame other people for your behavior and negative feelings; this one screams toxicity, especially if others are extracting these negative reactions from us. However, another cause for blaming others stems from our lack of maturity and inability to take responsibility.	The solution for dealing with this issue requires self-awareness at its core; here are some tips: 1. Take a minute to analyze what just occurred before rushing in to confront the situation. 2. Reflect on why you constantly feel numbed after you've blamed someone; this is where reflection comes in. Journaling is a great tool to incorporate. 3. Acknowledge that when we blame, it's usually caused by a lack of communication. 4. Try to shift the blame into constructive criticism instead.
You find yourself anxious about seeing someone or attending	The solutions for remedying this issue are as follows: 1. Talk to a therapist about your

WHY YOU MAY NEED BOUNDARIES

The Reason	The Boundary
certain social/workplace events. Certain people trigger this form of dread within us, and it's usually a result of not being comfortable in their presence. Maybe you don't agree with their opinion or the way they socialize. This can feel extremely problematic in workplace settings. This issue can result in serious social anxiety.	emotions, and they'll help you construct various coping mechanisms. 2. Explore with the therapist what your triggers are, and you will be able to source constructive coping strategies. 3. Always challenge your negative thoughts and remember that the mindset can be refocused. 4. Start small; results won't be immediate, but they'll emerge with consistency. 5. Role-play within a trusted support group; this will help ease and prepare you for eventual social situations.
You find yourself using unhealthy coping mechanisms during stressful situations.	The solution to preventing unhealthy mechanisms involves great self-awareness; here are some tips: 1. Start with your triggers. 2. Create a great and trusted support

WHY YOU MAY NEED BOUNDARIES	
The Reason	**The Boundary**
	group.
	3. Enhance your relationship with self-care.
	4. Set small goals to begin with.
	5. Exercise to boost your mood and health.
	6. Practice gratitude, and don't forget to journal each night and reflect on the three things you're most thankful for.
	7. Always celebrate your progress, regardless of how minor it may feel.

An important thing to note about the information clarified above is that most of the techniques and tips mentioned recur across several issues. In a later chapter, we'll discuss the beneficial qualities of constructing a self-care practice to incorporate all of these preventable techniques to ensure the sustainability of your boundaries. Now, it's totally common for us to set boundaries and find that they are no longer functional. This may surprise you, but the most common reason for them failing is due to your emotions. The issue is that we find ourselves rushing into establishing the boundary without fully considering the emotional work needed for it to succeed. Emotions are highly influential toward boundaries; this means that if we're creating a boundary from anger or sadness, the legitimacy of the emotion will negatively impact the success rate of the boundary.

Why Do Boundaries Fail, and Can You Fix an Existing Boundary?

Yes, you can fix an existing boundary. There are various reasons for the boundary failing, and usually the main reason is due to our emotions.

RE-ESTABLISHING YOUR BOUNDARIES	
The Emotion	**How to Fix It**
Resentment	Resentment is a complex emotion that arises from a variety of emotional issues, and often neither of us is actually aware of the cause of it. However, with boundaries, resentment usually arises because we find ourselves overcommitting and overextending our capabilities. For example, maybe you agreed to stay after hours to help a colleague with a project, maybe you're helping a friend study when conflicting with your own studies, or maybe you're trying to complete a work task while on holiday with your family—resentment usually arises from these sorts of activities. However, resentment serves as a good reminder for when you're crossing your own boundaries, so if feelings of frustration,

RE-ESTABLISHING YOUR BOUNDARIES	
The Emotion	**How to Fix It**
	disappointment, bitterness, or even sadness arise, check in with yourself and what you're feeling. A thing to note is that resentment has this ability to attach itself to others, meaning that we'd likely find ourselves blaming the other person or situation before holding ourselves accountable. Here are tips to manage resentment in relation to your boundary: • Reflect: If any feeling mimicking resentment arises, take a minute, find someplace private, and check in with yourself about what you're feeling. • Journal: Sometimes we're not able to identify the exactness of the emotions we're feeling, so turning to our journals is a great way of figuring out what's going on with you. • Work on establishing "no." We previously discussed various forms of establishing no. Work on them.
Dread	Dread is a type of anxiety; it's considered a free-floating emotion that consumes the body and mind upon the instant trigger. Free-falling is used to describe the floating sensation of anxiety and its ability to jump from thought to thought. Dread is a

RE-ESTABLISHING YOUR BOUNDARIES	
The Emotion	**How to Fix It**
	dismantling emotion; not only is it threatening, but it fills you with sickness. There are various reasons (triggers) for dread to arise; they can be as simple as a knock on the door, going to work, having to answer a call, or someone's choice of vocabulary.
	Dread problematizes boundaries because it strengthens that negative voice in the back of our heads, criticizing the choices and specifically the need for the boundary. Anxiety-based issues have a convincing way of undermining these issues. Here are some tips to help manage your boundary:
	• Always try to question your thought pattern to gain more clarity. Remember that most of the time, these thoughts arise from a negative space. When we question them, we're challenging them and ultimately regaining control.
	• Working on your breathing, taking a pause, and practicing mindful breathing go a long way and will ultimately help you calm down.
	• Stay active; not only will it impact your health, but it's going to positively affect your mental health, improve your sleep quality, and boost your

RE-ESTABLISHING YOUR BOUNDARIES	
The Emotion	**How to Fix It**
	mood.
Fatigue	Fatigue is a common issue, sabotaging boundaries. When we're overwhelmed with tiredness, it affects our daily functions, and completing tasks becomes an eventual hurdle. This unfortunately negatively affects our boundaries—setting a boundary is a task and, at the beginning, it's a constant accomplishment required each day. For example, if one of your boundaries is following a nutritious diet and you return home in the evening from an exhausting day at work, it may be easier to disregard the rule of the diet (the boundary). Or maybe you've just left the company of a friend and feel drained, tired, and overly critical of yourself; this is a sign that you crossed your boundary. We often miss this issue due to the belief that we must always be there for those closest to us, but there are limitations in support. Here are some tips to help you: • Eat nutritious meals because they're going to boost your immune system and ultimately allow you to function throughout the day. • Stick to your sleep schedule; let this be a boundary that no person or form of media crosses. Our brains require

RE-ESTABLISHING YOUR BOUNDARIES

The Emotion	How to Fix It
	sleep to initiate repair, and when our brains are up to par, we're capable of accomplishing our goals. • Limit your time with people by socializing in a group of three or more; this allows for a variety of opinions to flow within the group. It will curb the amount of energy you invest in the experience.
Hurt	Most of the time, we're not sure why we feel hurt after a conversation with someone. The difficulty with feeling hurt is that we can't always pinpoint why we feel it or what exactly led us to feel that way. Your current mindset won't associate the feeling of hurt with those in your company or anything beyond yourself. However, when you experience this feeling, it's a good step toward understanding that you need more personalized boundaries. Emotions have a way of hiding within us when they're not dealt with, so when we create boundaries, the hope is to locate what it is about these conversations that wound us so badly. Here are tips to help you: • Feel what you must before moving on; if you're going to dismiss your feelings, you're signing off on these

RE-ESTABLISHING YOUR BOUNDARIES	
The Emotion	**How to Fix It**
	feelings revisiting you in the future. • Communicate your feelings, particularly when you feel hurt by those around you. If you can't find the courage to do so, use your journal, and eventually, with time, you'll be able to build the confidence. • Reflect on whatever just happened; again, this can be done in the form of journaling.
Judgmental	Most of the time, when we're experiencing judgmentalism, it means that we're secretly jealous of what the other person is doing. For example, you may judge someone for being selfish or for being stuck up for following a specific diet and fitness program. It could even be them taking the time to learn a new skill, which involves them limiting their time with the group and socializing. Regardless of how you're judging them, it's usually a sign that you need a boundary. The truth is that there's no reason for you not to be achieving similar goals as those you are envious of; it just means that you need sturdier boundaries to see it through. Here are some tips to help you: • Always be mindful of your thought

RE-ESTABLISHING YOUR BOUNDARIES	
The Emotion	**How to Fix It**
	pattern; it's easy to get lost in a judgmental mindset and not an actionable one. • Always question your assumptions about the situation or experience; likely, you're simply blinded. • Recognize that you're being biased; each of us is different from the other, and there's no way you could know what someone is going through without proper conversation. • Be empathetic whenever you judge someone else; think about how you're feeling and how misinterpretation would make you feel. • Be positive. Journaling can help you with this tip; each night, list down three things that you are thankful for—this is going to help you practice gratitude.

How Do I Know If My Boundaries Are Healthy?

So, how does one establish healthy boundaries? The first step is understanding why the boundary is needed; this ultimately leads to creating healthier boundaries. Boundaries are defined as sustainable practices that need little force to maintain. Here's how to identify healthy boundaries:

1. You're able to use "no" freely and without feeling guilty.

2. You feel safe enough to express yourself and openly share your emotions without judgment.

3. You only ask for what you need and want.

4. You're in control of your own success and fulfillment of joy, so you reach for opportunities that benefit your life.

5. You're able to care for yourself and your emotions.

6. You're able to use "yes" without negativity or guilt because it's ultimately what you want.

7. You don't feel responsible for someone else's happiness or success, so you're never overwhelmed.

8. You're being treated as an equal because that's what your boundaries are demanding.

9. You are attuned to your emotions and live according to your values, beliefs, and opinions.

10. You respect yourself.

Chapter 2:

Healthy Boundaries:

Cultivating Self-Awareness and

Identifying Your Boundaries

I never could have done what I have done, without the habits of punctuality, order, and diligence, without the determination to concentrate myself on one object at a time. –Charles Dickens

The simplest way to ensure the health of a boundary (remember, there are several forms of boundaries that are present within our lives; we'll break them down in a minute) is with intention and honesty. Think of boundaries as psychological experiences that require the same care as emotional trauma or physical wounds. Now, by intention and honesty, I mean that when a boundary is created, you must acknowledge it, so that those around you respect it. The first thing to remember is that in order to establish any boundary, we need to have great self-awareness on the issue that necessitates the boundary. Once we have cultivated self-awareness, we're able to identify the parts of us that require change, and once we encourage this change (we'll elaborate on this in a minute), we'll promote self-development.

What is Self-Awareness?

Self-awareness is a form of deep and practiced reflection; it's about being aware—yes, literally aware—of the traits, behaviors, attitudes, feelings, character, and motives that define you. Self-awareness is a state; to some, it's a spiritual state that enables you to observe your surroundings and yourself in order to better understand yourself. The ultimate goal is to determine your desires and goals and intentionally move them toward accomplishment. When we're practicing self-awareness we're mindfully eliminating things (and even people, though we remove them in this regard) from our lives that offer us no success or joy. Being self-aware means that we're comfortable aligning our thoughts, actions, and emotions toward our goals and ultimately our prosperity. Here are some benefits of cultivating self-awareness:

1. You'll develop the ability to not only manage but also self-regulate your emotions. This positively affects your ability to communicate with others.

2. Your self-esteem will improve, allowing you to feel more confident and comfortable with yourself.

3. Your critical thinking skills will improve and affect your decision-making skills.

4. A sense of authenticity will develop, allowing you to better understand your values, goals, and needs.

5. You'll be more empathetic toward others.

6. You'll develop better self-control.

7. You'll experience a reduction in stress and anxiety levels.

According to Perry, there are two distinct types of self-awareness, public and private:

- Public self-awareness: This is about being aware of your environment and how you may appear to those around you. Though this improves your observation skills and socialization skills, the downside is that you become too self-aware of yourself within the public sphere.

- Private self-awareness: This is based on your internal feelings, allowing you the space to reflect before reacting while being able to fully understand your emotions and their relation to the environment (Perry, 2022, para.3).

How to Improve Self-Awareness	
Meditate	Meditation is key to promoting mindfulness. Mindfulness refers to the concept of living with intention and awareness of yourself in relation to the world. Meditation is a difficult process and will ultimately require a lot of patience. It's defined as an act of intense focus and is often cultivated through yoga and breathing practices. Here's what to do: • Do some research; in fact, there are guided practices (with a teacher) encouraging you to follow along. • You'll need a quiet spot, preferably a trusted spot that will allow you to relax with your eyes closed. • Another tool to employ is yoga, which ultimately makes us more aware of our

How to Improve Self-Awareness	
	body and breath.
Strengths and Weaknesses	A great thing to do is to recognize what your strengths and weaknesses are. Here's the thing, though, weakness doesn't define you, and it is capable of being improved upon. This is why learning new skills is important for your personal development. Also, by knowing what our strengths are, we'll not only know how to expand upon them but simultaneously feel confident about them.
Self-Reflect	It's easy to get lost in the working mechanisms of society and other people. When we don't value our time and personal health, we can get taken advantage of. Self-reflection (as has been encouraged) will make you aware of your emotions and hold you accountable for the goals you need to complete. It's best to check in at the end of the day, though, as you progress. Journaling can take place in the morning or even throughout the day.
Monitor Self-Talk	Don't let that voice in your head get away with saying all those cruel things. Remember that this voice is designed to criticize you; it's meant to damage your success. So, whenever that voice appears, take a minute to call it out, and feed it facts. For example, if you're experiencing social anxiety about going out with friends, acknowledge that you are anxious, and that the

How to Improve Self-Awareness	
	easiest thing is going out with your friends and not staying behind. Because giving into the voice and believing it will sabotage you in the long run.
Question Your Decisions	It's easy to believe that your decisions are the right ones, but even with great self-awareness you must question every decision. This allows us to further explore self-awareness and emotional regulation while optioning the decision from various points of view.

Does Self-Awareness Enable Positive Boundaries?

Yes, it does, because when we develop the ability to self-regulate our emotions, we're able to view our decisions and selves from various perspectives. Boundaries are about cultivating trust and respect and developing our communication skills. Because as much as the boundary is about us, it is more important to those who must respect it.

A Case Study about Tom

Tom felt that he no longer had a personal life and had fallen into the habit of going out for drinks with colleagues after work (a regular nine to five). The regularity made Tom realize that doing this day after day felt like an extra shift; it felt like work. Worst of all, weekends were used to catch up on sleep (actually, there's no such thing as catching up on sleep, and we'll discuss this in a later chapter). Let's be clear, the phrase "catch up" is inappropriate and shouldn't exist within your vocabulary, especially when it's used in relation to family and friends. Tom had had enough and felt that he wasted his time, especially on weekends, and declared that he would no longer have drinks with colleagues. However, Tom was unaware of the amount of work required to create this boundary. Tom strived for balance and ultimately wanted to remove the words *catch up* and *schedule*—and the sensations they evoked—from his personal life. Though Tom appeared successful at the start, he'd spend the evening eating by himself, sometimes ordering in, and bingeing a new TV series. He found that he had more time to do his laundry and tidy up properly after himself. However, there was a noticeable change in his mood; he felt fatigued most days and sometimes just bored, and he still found himself sleeping in on weekends.

See if you can answer these for me:

- Why was Tom fatigued despite having more free time?

- Tom stopped doing negative things, meaning that he disliked staying out with his colleagues, so why was he unhappy?

- If he had more time for himself, why was he still sleeping in on weekends?

- He seemed productive, cleaning his apartment, and doing the laundry, so why was he fatigued?

- What is wrong with this boundary?

Though Tom's intentions were good, he seemingly discarded research on how boundaries worked or how to cultivate healthy ones. Most people have the habit of streamlining into the concept of change, believing that when they stop doing one thing (like going out at night), it is the equivalent of change and creating a boundary. It's not—without proper intention and rules, this version of a boundary will eventually wither.

- Tom was tired because his daily chores required a lot of effort and energy, and it's likely that his diet was unhealthy. He spent his free time avoiding people or social experiences that required his participation outside.

- Because Tom decided to "stop" as opposed to change his behavior, he stripped himself of social connections. For example, he should have approached the situation slowly; it's easier to reduce your staying-out time as opposed to removing that time slot entirely. I do think that this is an important factor; in fact, I highly encourage you to approach the concept of change slowly—that old saying that goes one step at a time is wholesome advice. This will help you better understand your need for the reduction—the boundary—while also allowing you the space to understand what self-care means (we'll discuss self-care in more depth a bit later) and how influential it could be.

- Tom likely continued to sleep in because his body had been scheduled and his mental health had conditioned him this way. Be mindful that negative environmental experiences influence our mental health.

Psychological Change

According to Aakash, "Psychological change refers to the process of altering an individual's thoughts, emotions, and behaviors. It involves shifting one's perspective, beliefs, and habits to achieve a desired outcome" (Aakash, n.d., para.2). Psychological change is directly aimed at adapting your psychological processes; these processes are also referred to as mental processes and comprise our five basic processes:

sensation, perception, memory, attention, and learning. Psychological change often occurs due to therapy, self-reflection techniques, or life events. However, they ultimately serve to empower the individual and help them make more positive changes to their lives (Aakash, n.d., para. 2). Here are some benefits of change:

- You're going to develop personal growth.

- You're going to become more comfortable with flexibility.

- You're going to feel more motivated and this will improve your confidence and compassion.

- It's going to enhance your lifestyle and open you up to new opportunities.

- It's going to cultivate healthy connections.

Examples of Psychological Change

- Learning new skills and expanding your knowledge: By continuing to learn, it alters the way we perceive and understand the world and ultimately leads to us improving our decision-making skills and behavior.

- Changing your belief or attitude: This is encouraged by new information; it possesses the ability to alter our beliefs and attitudes successfully.

- Coping with trauma: Going through a traumatic experience causes us to reevaluate our place in the world; coping with it allows our emotions and thoughts to change.

- New habits: Habits develop due to consistency, and healthy habits can improve our overall well-being.

- Therapy: New perspectives and insights are found when we seek therapy; this leads to a change in behaviors, thought processes, and new emotions.

- Recovering from addiction: Recovery comprises a range of psychological changes which include the development of coping mechanisms, changing thought patterns, and building new habits (Aakash, n.d., para. 4).

Therefore, we must pursue the idea of being comfortable with the feeling of discomfort because that's the only way you're going to get through this situation. Something else to keep in mind is that the feelings that arise when change is evoked have nothing to do with you personally. In fact, I'm certain that change might have been evoked around you, and naturally, you reacted poorly (and this might have been internally). Change just happens to be one of those movements that complicates our feelings.

Society tends to create this narrative that if we're open with people, if we share everything there is to know about ourselves with them, they are able to understand our deepest desires. This isn't true; the self—yours and mine—is so intricately woven into our psyches that we barely know how to identify ourselves. A good support system is always nice to have, but even those support systems (no fault of their own) can misunderstand us. So, when change is introduced to our narratives, it unfortunately affects someone else's narrative—this is simply because we are creatures of (and informed by) habit.

Habits are considered learned behaviors that ultimately become unconscious behaviors; this is why bad habits are so concerning. Usually, when change is evoked it means that a habit is changing; however, this doesn't necessarily mean that it's a bad habit changing. It can be as simple as switching jobs or moving to a new place or city—any unconscious behavior being changed is met with defense mechanisms, and this is why people react poorly sometimes. It's likely that they're used to our habit or that our habit would inform their own with change, regardless of how you look at it. The thing is, change is unwelcome because it means that you and those around you are going to have to unlearn and relearn new behaviors.

We are each consumed with good and bad habits, and bad habits could easily be a lack of exercise, smoking, biting your nails, or having caffeine too late in the evening. However, habits can be changed and even developed into boundaries.

Should You Change Every Bad Habit?

Yes, but this isn't possible. The frightening thing about bad habits is how unconscious and deeply buried they are within us and our psyche. In fact, we're so reliant on the bad habit that we're never fully conscious of it being fulfilled. This is why it's important to be aware of your habits, whether they're good or bad. Your brain naturally relies on unconscious behaviors as a way of getting through the day. So, it's unlikely that you'll be rid of bad habits. Another way bad habits are often overlooked is due to their association with coping mechanisms. For example, cracking your knuckles or biting your fingernails is more than just a habit and can be associated with anxiety or some form of coping mechanism. However, I do suggest that when it comes to breaking bad habits, the goal shouldn't be to remove them or attempt to eradicate them, but to constructively switch them into a better habit. According to Harvard Health Publishing, habits can be forged to our advantage if a particular three-step pattern is followed.

The Three Rs

The three-step pattern, also known as the three Rs pattern, is a way of recognizing whether a habit is good or bad. The goal is to identify how they affect your life—remember that a good habit influences self-improvement whereas a bad habit might be binge-watching a TV series as opposed to getting enough sleep. On the surface, it might not seem like a bad habit, and I'm not suggesting that you should stop binge-watching TV (I do this too), but bad habits are sneaky and shouldn't overstep our health or, in this instance, sleep (Star Health Publishing, 2016, paras 1-4).

Another example could be not drinking enough water when one of your boundaries (and self-care practices) revolves around your diet and health. Health is an optimal practice for success. We know that regular exercise affects our health and therefore will inform our mental health, and when our mental health is functional, we're in a safe space to create, learn, and achieve our goals.

Reminder	Routine	Reward

Healthy boundaries need healthy habits to succeed. However, when it comes to switching bad habits for good ones, change is required. In fact, this entire process—the establishment of boundaries—is reliant on change, and as we said, success begins with getting comfortable with the uncomfortable. However, something that often gets lost in the conversation about change is the concept of confidence and motivation. Many times I meet people who are so willing and so excited about turning their lives around, but when the actual process starts, they begin to falter.

Change is difficult, it is frightening, and many people often falter under the pressure of seeing the process through. It's okay not to want to disrupt someone else's life. But this is why confidence and motivation are extremely important; these two sensations possess the ability to strengthen your mindset. When we feel good about ourselves, we're able to accomplish our goals a bit more easily (Harvard Health Publishing, 2016, paras 5-7).

So, simply put, when you're about to change a habit, it's best to ask yourself how committed you are, because some habits are harder than others. I think that drinking an extra glass of water is easier than reducing your cigarette intake by one each day. I'd suggest that you make a list of both your good and bad habits and do your best to list them all. The next step involves the three Rs, which, I confess, might seem complicated at first, but trust me, the process works. The first step requires you to choose one of the bad habits. I'd personally go with the smallest or one that could be considered the easiest to change. I suggest this because building confidence is tricky, and a great hack is to build up confidence with actions we know are achievable. So, once you've chosen a habit, you'll begin to apply the three Rs:

- A reminder aims to identify the triggers that initiate this behavior.

- The routine aims to clarify what action then proceeds after the trigger is identified.

- Reward aims to showcase how the behavior is then compensated.

According to Harvard Health Publishing, this (the three Rs) results in a continuous loop and presents the following example: You have the habit of eating junk food while watching TV late at night. If your loop begins at 9 p.m. with your TV show, this becomes the reminder. Your next step involves you heading into the kitchen for a snack, and this becomes the routine. The reward would be you enjoying that snack while you're watching your TV show. Sure, this doesn't seem bad. It's totally normal for us to curl up on the sofa with a snack while watching a TV show. The reason we investigate each habit and its cycle within the sphere of the three Rs is not only to discover if the habit is negative but also to learn a bit more about ourselves (Harvard Health Publishing, 2016, para 8).

This particular loop recurs daily throughout your life; it's only fair to ask yourself why this loop occurs. Junk food has a bad reputation, but that doesn't mean you have to remove all treats from your life to be healthy. Health is about balance. Here's another issue with bad habits: If (still following the example above) you're stuck in this loop and eating unhealthy food each day, the obvious step to change is to remove the junk food, right? Sure, but it's unlikely that this will work. Remember, removing bad habits is difficult; the goal should be to reduce them and hopefully turn them into good habits because the issue here isn't necessarily the food but the habit.

So, once you have investigated your habit, the next step is to review it. Harvard Health Publishing instructs us to review the reminder and routine. The aim is to understand why these two concepts occur. For example, if you're heading into the kitchen at 9 p.m. every night, stop and ask yourself why you're doing this. It's recommended to start a list of words or phrases to describe what your feelings are in relation to this action. First, begin by exploring what you're feeling before this action begins—are you hungry, bored, or tired? Second, when this action is in effect, ask yourself the same question—how do you feel?—and note down every word that comes up. The next step is to locate your triggers. Research has broken down the concept of triggers into five categories (Harvard Health Publishing, 2016, para. 12). Here they are:

- Location would take place in the living room (in this example, we're in the living room on the sofa watching TV).

- Time is 9 p.m.

- Emotional state is dependent on those words you listed; let's go with boredom in this case.

- Exterior accounts for other people in your vicinity; in this example, there are none around.

- Immediate precedence before action explores what you did before this loop began and you were rewarded; in this regard, it begins with your TV show beginning.

These five categories might seem odd, but they are a great way of narrowing down your feelings. Another thing to note is that you would have to follow this pattern for a few days before better understanding the choices you've made. After about three to five days, gather your information and review it. It could be that your snack is dependent on whether or not you're alone, how late you're watching TV, or if you're in a particular mood. Honestly, there are a variety of reasons why you're snacking; the goal is to try and narrow down its specificity for occurring so that you're able to switch this habit into a healthier one. It could be that you're snacking because you're stressed, it's due to a lack of sleep, or your anxiety is creeping.

Another thing to note is that snacking late while watching TV won't be considered a bad habit for everyone. However, for someone who is an insomniac or someone who wants to follow a particular diet or wants to lose weight, this can be considered a bad habit. Knowing what your triggers are impacts your overall success, especially your ability to achieve your goals. The next step is about boosting your motivation; this requires you to draw up an additional list of the types of rewards you enjoy. The point of listing the kinds of rewards you enjoy is to allow them to positively influence healthier habits. For example, if you're a person who wants to lose weight or snack more healthily, the best approach to positively affecting your diet and habits would be to choose healthier snacks (Harvard Health Publishing, 2016, para. 13).

I want to be clear about my usage of the word "healthier." I believe that it is a controversial word, and I don't want to suggest that eating an apple is a healthier alternative to eating chocolate. Often, the healthier choice could be the one with fewer calories or something that's nutrient-dense like a superfood. I have a friend who switches potato chips for popcorn due to the calorie intake. Another example could be replacing late-night binge-watching with meditation or reading. The point is that there's always an alternative, and by listing the things we enjoy, we're boosting our self-esteem with pleasure and not feeling bad about ourselves for possibly staying up too late and snacking unhealthily.

The truth is, the best relationship you're ever going to be able to have is with yourself. So, once you've gone through the process of examining your routine and the triggers and figured out your rewards, you should be able to break the loop of the cycle and switch those bad habits into good ones. Be mindful of your behavior. For example, if you find that you're prone to snacking late at night, perhaps try to change the hours or days you watch TV or alternate between reading, meditation, or whatever other action is of interest to you. Remember, it's going to take time.

The Need for Self-Development

Boundaries are crucial because they impact our self-development. Many people overlook the idea of self-development as an action or process that requires intense concentration or consciousness. Or that one has to willingly choose to pursue self-development. This is a semi-true concept; however, the reality is that where we are conscious, we are also unconscious. The subconscious, or unconscious, mind is always working, and if we're not mindful about our self-development, the self ends up developing without our input. Consider this, if you're not mindful of the behaviors you're learning or becoming reliant on, bad habits can form without your consent. This is my point about society creating this narrative that self-development is supposedly only chosen and always only a good thing. If you're not careful, you are picking up bad habits and giving yourself double the work to rectify them.

Self-development takes time and dissuades many from seeing the process through, but its results are gradual and based on consistency. In fact, it's considered to be a lifelong process that's actioned by intentional thinking. Now, intentional thinking is another word for mindfulness, and mindfulness means to be actively aware of your surroundings both internally and externally. Remember, if you're intentional about the things you do, bad habits won't necessarily sneak up on you. For example, seeking out practices to help with your insomnia, as opposed to staying up and binge-watching, intentionally informs your health and well-being. Another way of defining self-development is by accepting it as the constant pursuit of personal growth.

Chapter 3:

How to Communicate with Boundaries

We all require devotion to something more than ourselves for our lives to be endurable. —Atul Gawande

The success of the boundary is reliant on effective communication; however, communication goes beyond verbal talk. It encapsulates a series of behaviors like active listening, pausing, and observing the body language of the other person. Also, active listening is about understanding the tonal element present in the voice.

Why Is Communication Important to Boundaries?

Once we understand the need for boundaries, the next step requires us to present these boundaries to those around us. Communicating is difficult to accurately convey on any given day, so being able to not only concisely share your boundaries but also confidently express them to people is important. By asserting confidence, we're (while being respectful) demanding that those around us respect the need for boundaries and ourselves.

What Prohibits Us from Active Listening?

The common issues that prohibit effective communication are:

- Stress and complex emotions: Feeling overwhelmed, stressed, or emotional blinds us to the emotions of those around us, allowing us to misunderstand the emotions and situations present.

  o If during a conversation you feel overwhelmed, excuse yourself for a minute and find a safe space to breathe and reflect on what you're feeling.

- Unable to focus: This distracts us from the situation at present, which ultimately causes misunderstandings and possible conflict.

  o When in conversation, put away your phone or stop what you're doing to respect the person.

- Inconsistent body language: This occurs when the person talking displays conflicting body language, which contributes to confusion and misunderstanding about the seriousness or truth of what is being said.

  o Remember that you can't say "yes" if you're shaking your head "no".

- Negative body language: When we dislike or disagree with what is said, we tend to display this with damaging body language that causes the other person to become defensive, for example, crossing their arms, tapping their feet, or modifying commentary.

o   Minding your body language goes a long way;
the smallest of details, like rolling your eyes, can
trigger someone.

How Do You Become Effective at Communication?

It's possible to improve your communication abilities; here are
some tips:

1. Be an active listener: According to Cuncic, "active
   listening is a communication skill" (Cuncic, 2022, para.
   1). It serves to help us better understand the emotion
   being used within language, requiring us to fully engage
   in the conversation.

SIX ACTIVE LISTENING TECHNIQUES	

Be Present	Take the time to focus on the speaker, the language, and body language being used. This serves to better inform us of what's happening in relation to the speaker. Here are some tips to help you:
	
	 • Do:
	
	    o Put away your phone and turn off the TV.
	
	    o Move to a quiet or less distracting space.

SIX ACTIVE LISTENING TECHNIQUES

	o Be mindful of your internal monologue. • Avoid: o Checking your phone. o Looking around too much. o Steer clear of overthinking. o Asking irrelevant questions.
Eye Contact	When we're using eye contact, it lets the other person know that we are present, that they are seen and heard, and that we ultimately respect them. However, be mindful of your gaze; if it's too eager or deadpan, it will dissuade the speaker. • Do: o The 50/70 rule involves you holding eye contact for about 50 to 70 percent of the time, so hold eye contact for about five seconds before looking away briefly.
Ask Questions	This shows the reader that you are engaged in the conversation and allows for flow and contemplation. Remember to ask open-ended questions; they're not only encouraging but can also promote positivity.

	SIX ACTIVE LISTENING TECHNIQUES

	• Do:
	
	    o Can you explain that to me a bit more?
	
	    o What do you think is the best way forward?
	
	    o How do you feel about that?
	
	• Avoid:
	
	    o Steer clear of yes or no questions, or at least don't rely on them too much.

Reflect	This is a great technique; when the speaker has finished, simply repeat what the person has said (based on your understanding) to them. This not only proves that you were listening but also that you want to accurately understand what they are going through.
	
	• Do:
	
	    o Ask for clarification.
	
	    o Summarize the information and present it to the speaker for accuracy.
	
	    o Use statements like "I'm hearing that you are frustrated," or, "From

	my perspective, you seem frustrated. Is this accurate?" • Avoid: o Focusing on insignificant details.

Be Patient	Let the person talk without interruption; this showcases your maturity, patience, and care for them and the situation. Remember that sharing information is personal and difficult for most of us.
	
	• Do:
	
	    o Let them finish the sentence before interjecting.
	
	• Avoid:
	
	    o Interruptions, don't try to finish their sentences.

Don't Judge	The minute we begin to judge or apply criticism to the person, we tear down the "safe space." As previously mentioned, most of us need time and comfort to share. Judging someone will create toxicity and discomfort and prevent the person from wanting to share with you again. Here are some tips: • Be empathetic.

SIX ACTIVE LISTENING TECHNIQUES	
	• Practice acceptance.
	• Be mindful.
	• Pause and reflect before responding.

2. Pay attention to non-verbal cues: Body language accompanies speech; observe the look and movement of the other person to better comprehend what is being said and felt. Nonverbal communication comprises of:

- Body language

- Body movement

- Facial expressions

- Gestures

- Eye contact

- Posture

- Tone of voice

- Muscle tension

- Breathing

Identifying these nonverbal communications in others will help you self-identify them within you, which will help you express yourself and navigate through challenging conversations. An effective way of using nonverbal communication is through open body language—this means that we forgo closed or defensive types of gestures. Open body language is a great tool to employ when discussing our boundaries with people.

- Choose to gesture with uncrossed arms and an open stance, or sit at the edge of your seat (literally) and engage in the conversation.

- Open body language can also be used as an emphasis on the verbal language used, for example, with a hug, smile, or the light tapping of a shoulder.

Here's how to improve your reading of nonverbal communication:

- Keep in mind that nonverbal communication gestures vary between people. This is due to many factors like culture, religion, race, nature vs. nurture principles, age, and emotional maturity. Be patient and observant.

- Don't focus on a singular gesture, but rather on the collection of nonverbal communication gestures that the person is using. It's normal for someone to unconsciously change their body language without meaning anything by it, so focus on the collection and the person.

Here's how to improve your delivery of nonverbal communication:

- Make sure that your words and nonverbal gestures match: You shouldn't be nodding your head or shrugging your shoulders if you're saying "no." The listener will feel confused or even draw suspicious conclusions.

- Appropriately adjust your nonverbal gestures depending on subject and person: Your tone of voice should alter between individuals; for example, speaking to a child differs from speaking to an adult.

3. Monitor stress levels: If left unchecked, they will run wild and lead you toward mental exhaustion and burnout. A common problem with stress is that regardless of where the emotion starts, it occupies every other aspect of our lives, sabotaging progress. A great way to manage stress is by crafting a calm space within you, because it's only when we're calm that we're able to determine the best way to approach the situation. Here's what to do if you're feeling stressed:

  - Stall: To allow yourself time to think, ask questions, even if it means having the question repeated before you respond.

  - Pause: Check in with yourself before; this is going to allow you to feel more in control.

  - Make one point: By saying or asking one thing only, you limit the risk of overexplaining, overtalking, or fumbling over your words.

  - Speak clearly: Maintain eye contact and even out your tone as you speak, and also make sure your body language is relaxed.

  - End with a summary: Simply summarize your response and stop talking; don't mind the silence it might cause.

However, sometimes we find ourselves suddenly drawn into heated conversations, which end up spiking our stress levels.

IF THINGS ARE HEATED, HERE'S WHAT TO DO	
Recognize	Firstly, your body will let you know that something's happening and that you're stressed. Despite how universal stress is for each of us, its symptoms might vary. For example, your body might tense up and twitch, or maybe your stomach clenches or your jaw snaps. Whatever's happening, note it down in your memory as a sign that you're stressed.
Calm Down	This may be the hardest thing to do, but it is necessary, and the best way to do this is to walk away from the situation. Find a safe space and reflect on your emotions before returning.
Use Your Senses	This allows you to return to your surroundings. Stress has the habit of isolating the mind, so be mindful of the sounds, smells, tastes, sights, and touch in proximity to you in order to ground yourself.
Negativity	Though you should be positive and respectful about your emotions, it's totally fine to express your anger or frustration; just be mindful of the emotions of those around you.
Positivity	Whether it's compliments or criticism, be respectful of the feedback.
Say "No"	Respect your limits; it's easy to be taken

advantage of if you're not mindful of yourself.

4. Assert Yourself: Boundaries require directness, which in turn will boost your confidence and self-esteem because you're ultimately championing yourself. However, note that assertiveness is not the equivalent of rudeness or forcefulness; it's about expressing your values and boundaries to your peers. Here are ways to improve your assertiveness:

- Value yourself and your opinions; don't let anyone make you feel as if you or your opinion are not important.

- Respect your needs and wants, and learn how to express them to those around you without negatively hindering their own.

- Reflect on your negative thoughts. Journaling is a great way to understand and accept your emotions.

- Be positive about the feedback you receive; don't take it personally.

- Be comfortable with saying "no."

Chapter 4:

Self-Care and Boundaries

The art of life lies in a constant readjustment to our surroundings. —
Kakuzo Okakura

Self-care is likened to a notable skill that each individual should acquire to live a more successful life. It's a brilliant association because the boundary ultimately aims to protect the practice (self-care). Remember, a skill is your ability to do a particular thing well; anything can become a skill if learned and executed with motivation. Now, if the characteristics and attributes that make up our individuality were viewed as skills (and remember, skills can be upskilled), the road toward success would be in clear view, right? I want to be clear about my usage of the word success.

Success is about accomplishing a specific goal you set for yourself. Modernism has saturated the idea (and its pressure) of success into our subconscious fibers; this version of success expects us to constantly exploit our well-being to reach the peak of success. I know what you're thinking—when did the idea of success become so intense? I suppose a simple way of answering this is by acknowledging that we allowed society—a collection of figures informed by technology, capitalism, and consumerism—to define basic principles (alongside success, it's happiness, love, spiritualism, and even mental health) for ourselves. And yes, this is due to a lack of boundaries, but I don't think that it's anyone's direct fault; society, or rather, societal opinion, possesses the natural ability to overwhelm the individual.

This is another boundary that is often overlooked; many aren't aware that boundaries should extend into the realm of society or be directed at society—I don't mean come directly with fists at society (we're pacifists here), but only to hold society accountable for its actions. The case for this is simply that many of us don't assume that society warrants that much effect over our lives or that because society's involvement in our lives doesn't feel physical, its negativity is of lesser evil. This brings to our attention the notion that boundaries should extend internally and that our mindsets should be prioritized as well. Mental health is extremely important when it comes to maintaining boundaries, and we'll discuss this in the next chapter. First, we'll continue discussing boundaries and self-care pairs. Let's discuss the practice of self-care and skills and how a lack of boundaries is detrimental to our well-being.

What is Self-Care Exactly?

It goes by various names; you can call it a practice, a ritual, a skill, or a routine. Self-care is a compilation or a collection of actions that aims to ensure your well-being. The practice, which is known as a skill, varies between people, meaning that what works for me won't work for you. This is strictly because no individual is the same. An example of this could be diet. Someone might prioritize a specific dietary choice, maybe as a vegan or the keto diet, and this choice of diet would classify itself as a self-care practice. Another infamous self-care practice is morning and evening routines. These aim to prioritize the self and either help prepare the self for the day or help the self wind down before bed. Both of these are equally important constructs. Self-care is extremely trendy in society; however, when you're approaching the practice, do so with precision.

Morning and evening routines might not be your thing, or rather, they don't need to be as extreme as the next person. Remember to use the internet in an intelligent way. Aestheticism regarding the idea of self-care swarms the internet, and the last thing you should be doing is mimicking or building yours because someone else's routine looks pretty. Ultimately, self-care means taking care of yourself. Now, to be more precise, the self is everything you are as a whole; it's your mentality, characteristics, attributes, personality, and consciousness. And the ideal point of seeking out a care practice (self-care) is basically to feed those components of you with healthy regimens. For example, if you suffer from an anxiety disorder, one of your self-care practices should aim to care for your overall mentality. The same goes for insomnia. To care for your mental health, self-care should focus on the prioritization of sleep.

So, when it comes to browsing the internet for practices to follow, be mindful of what those practices demand and request from you. Though sleep should be prioritized for each of us, it's not necessary for a non-insomniac person to follow an insomniac's schedule and preparation for sleep. Same goes for diet; the ultimate goal should be to eat healthily within the sphere of balance, so it shouldn't be necessary for you to become vegan or limit yourself to a harsh diet just for the sake of it. Note that when we're approaching a self-care practice from a place of mindfulness and commitment, optimal health is achievable. Intention goes a long way and honestly saves you double the work in the long haul. So, my advice is to always practice intentionality.

Does Self-Care Work for Everyone?

Well, the short answer is yes; self-care *can* work for everyone. We just spoke about the power of intentionality; if a person lacks this, the choices they're making in relation to their goals will face challenges. Now, this isn't to say that if you're intentional, there won't be any challenge; of course not. Life is tough, and living is made up of challenges. This is why we employ boundaries to help us navigate these spaces. Let's start small. What is intention, or intentionality? It stems from a philosophical background that defines the quality of your mental state when it's directed toward an object, person, or experience. Living with intention, or intentionality, is basically living with self-awareness.

Being intentional means being deliberate and specific. So, if you're committing to a forty-five-minute evening routine every night, the best thing that you can do for yourself is to be intentional about it, which will eventually lead to the maintenance of boundaries. Remember, everything we do works in a loop. But in order for this loop to work smoothly, we must ensure that our mindsets are actively pursuing their goals, or rather, we must be honest with ourselves about what we want. I stumbled on this quote by Maya Angelou the other day. She said that if you're not clear about the things you want from life, you deserve everything you get from it. This is true and also my point, and it speaks toward the idea of being intentional.

I often find that many people are always ready to complain about their circumstances and lives. I know that living is difficult, and by no means am I suggesting that refocusing your mindset will save you from a difficult situation. Maya Angelou says that when we approach the idea of making decisions mindlessly we shouldn't then complain about the outcome we've received. I think the same goes for goals; we tend to shrug off setbacks and failure and are always ready to offer excuses. I've been in this situation before, and I know what it's like to suddenly make a series of decisions only to see them crumble days later. This, I realized, was due to a lack of intentionality.

Remember that intentionality is based on honesty, and don't misunderstand me; you should always try to be honest with people, especially those around you. If you're interested in improving your wind-down time in the evening, or if you're interested in relaxing, then be honest about it because not everyone will understand why you need forty-five minutes to yourself in the evening. But we spoke about change and how it impacts the lives of those around us. An interesting benefit of living with intentionality is that it refines purpose and meaning for yourself.

What Are the Benefits of Living with Intentionality?

Remember that this journey requires small steps; rushing into things won't speed up the process. Our overall goal is to create boundaries, but boundaries are ultimately walls, right? I described them as barriers, and their purpose is to protect our self-care practices. Now, I also introduced the concept of a loop, and I want to address the usage of this concept. In order for us to create functional self-care practices, we must be intentional about the things that we're passionate about— things that our soul is passionate about. So, when we're intentional, we're being honest, and honesty creates the practices we incorporate into self-care. And once we're able to name these self-care practices, we are able to wrap a boundary around each of them.

So, the first step is practicing intentionality, and yes, sometimes it's complicated. But it's doable; being intentional about things removes the action of navigating through daily life on autopilot. However, one thing to note is that autopilot isn't an entirely negative process; our brains rely on autopilot for many important reasons. But, yes, it's problematic when autopilot provides no essential benefits to our well-being. When we're living with intentionality, our time and energy are maximized and specific. Here are some significant benefits of living with intentionality.

Purpose and Meaning

Modernity says that everything we do must carry traces of purpose and meaning. The phrase that life is short and possibly wasted (if not watched) circles our emotional growth; if we're not careful, it limits our overall growth. Though I agree with the concept of infusing purpose and meaning into our actions, I unfortunately know that it's complicated and nearly impossible to enforce into our mindsets. There's a lot of background noise from society that tends to wear us down, and there's not enough conversation around the proper principles needed to enforce purpose and meaning. I'll be honest with you; I'm not entirely sure where our life's purpose comes from or how we gain meaning from it. I do think that purpose comes before meaning and that the latter can only be had once the former is reached.

I stumbled on a video interview by a musician who described his youth as a difficult place that had no space or affordability for music. He claimed to have spent his youth without the impression of music and only stumbled into it years later when his friends began to pursue music. But even then, while his friends were writing and making beats, he was just on the sidelines, unable to properly understand the format and the work that creating music required. Beside him was another musician who vibrated with music; the other musician understood the language and the work and basically lived for music. These two people are friends; the more experienced musician encouraged the other to pursue music too and offered to teach him.

Both musicians are remarkably successful, but my point here is that the first musician didn't start off with this purpose. The other musician did, though; from an early age, music was breath and blood to him, and ultimately his purpose. So, I don't think that we're necessarily born with this purpose, and you don't have to feel bad if you don't know what your purpose in life is. I know that life seems to speed along, and that if we're not safely strapped in, we're going to miss out on opportunity. But going along with things just for the sake of it doesn't provide you with any benefits; all it does is remove intentionality from your mindset.

Stress and Anxiety

Your stress and anxiety levels will significantly reduce because we're employing prioritization, which simply helps us do away with things that don't positively serve to benefit our overall health. Also, less stress and anxiety create a safe and calmer space. Now, anxiety differs for each of us (honestly, everything differs between us), but it can be more intense. I do think that society creates a specific, maybe even more tone-deaf version of anxiety, and by this, I mean that the version of anxiety that gets passed around is lesser. My point is that I am aware that for some of us, anxiety is more complicated and requires medication, and if you are battling any form of it or mental illness, I encourage you to seek help. However, know that there is power when we're intentional, especially when we're going through challenging experiences. So, when we're practicing intentionality in relation to reducing stress and anxiety, we can choose to eliminate situations and people that are known to increase these conflicts within us. Basically, if it offers you no joy or fulfillment, remove it from your life; it's going to be so amazing for your mentality.

Clarity and Focus

You'll develop an improvement in your clarity and focus, and this will help you prioritize your goals:

- Your critical thinking skills will improve and will help you make better decisions.

- You're going to be in a better and safer space mentally, and this will reduce levels of anxiety and depression.

- You're going to want to succeed, open up to challenges, and develop a more determined attitude.

Your Self-Care Practices Will Improve

Now, we've already discussed how intentionality helps us locate and refine the practices we choose to classify as self-care. Remember, when it comes to defining self-care and constructing a practice, the choices we're making are based on the self—in its broad sense.

Your Relationships Will Improve

Being intentional about our time and energy influences our relationships. I do think that people overlook the fact that intentionality should be applied to relationships; most of us become so comfortable within relationships that we don't allow ourselves the possibility of the other person changing. This factors into the overall issue of change and people, and why we easily become defensive. When we view our relationships with people with a lack of clarity, we are unaware of the connections being broken. We know that relationships need care, love, and most importantly, time. Relationships function on interaction, and realizing this after the fact only made me feel worse.

The little things make all the difference, though, and I wholeheartedly mean this. Interacting with the people we care about is fundamental to our overall well-being. Socialization is an important practice to prioritize; it may seem odd, but scheduling dates with friends and family ultimately helps the process. When we're intentional about the placement of relationships in our lives, we're able to narrow down which should be removed. This might sound harsh, but we don't always have a clear perspective on the negative or toxic people in our lives.

Letting go of people is a difficult thing, but the reality of the situation is that when negativity is present in our lives, it bogs down our emotional functionality. We're not meant to thrive in negative environments, nor should we be comfortable or confident around toxic people. You might have heard the phrase "energy vampires" before. It basically means what it says, that there are people who are literal energy vampires roaming about in the world and latching on to us. I've had a couple, and honestly, removing them from my life was the best thing for my overall health. Therefore, when it comes to the power of intentional living, I'm always encouraging people to follow this principle; it honestly benefits you in so many ways.

The Health of Your Boundaries Will Strengthen

Intentionality boosts mentality; consider that everything you're doing is in direct relation to yourself. Basically, there's no room for negativity or wasted time. When our values are aligned with our mindset, making decisions and problem-solving is easier. However, the great benefit of this is that you won't feel overwhelmed or guilty about having to do something that doesn't align with your values. Remember that boundaries are barriers and are fueled by positivity. Hear me out—I know that when it comes to the idea and even the morals of positivity, the first things that pop into people's heads are affirmations and determined optimism. This isn't entirely wrong, but I do think that society tends to make things slightly superficial.

Our brains rely on a positive mindset to successfully manage any form of situation or experience. Because positivity begets productivity, and productivity is fueled by self-talk. I mean, it's pretty straightforward; if your mindset is negative, you're not going to accomplish much, are you? The idea of failure will destroy your mood. However, positivity in the form of healthy self-talk is motivating. Remember, self-talk is an automated stream of thoughts that flows through our heads. Also, positivity doesn't mean that you ignore or disregard the reality of the situation, especially when things are going bad. No, it means that you simply rely on logic, reason, and kinder words—remember, you are ultimately speaking to yourself. The goal of positive self-talk is to disallow the presence of negativity and have it filter your perspective. So, when it comes to the health of your boundaries, positivity is the nutrient-strengthening force.

Your Physical Health Will Improve

Now, your physical health, in relation to your intentionality, will improve if you're interested in improving your health. Boundaries protect what we value, and if you're passionate about fitness or diet, a well-established boundary will make sure that you're positively moving toward those goals. A thing to note about health is that it's a system that is integrated into other systems, meaning that if you're getting enough and proper sleep, your brain will function better. For example, if you're a poor sleeper and experience bouts of fatigue during the day, it's unlikely that you're going to be able to maintain your goals, especially if you're passionate about getting to the gym or eating a particular diet. Health is integrated into every other pillar you have.

If you're eating the rainbow (which is literally advised by nutritionists), your body will reap its benefits. The same goes for superfoods. I know that there's a lot of debate regarding the value of superfoods, but what makes them so special is that they're densely sourced with nutritional value. Being intentional about your health will reduce stress levels and improve your confidence because you'll end up feeling good both internally and externally.

You'll Be More Present

We spoke about the brain's ability to tap into autopilot. Society has this habit of stating that if we're not locked and loaded into a nine-to-five and working overtime, we won't be or reach the peak of success. It's almost ironic, isn't it? Think of the many successful people sharing their self-care practices, and really inspect the things they're saying and the places they're saying them from. I'm not here to disparage anyone's success or practice, but I don't think it's realistic to believe that each of us should view those successful practices and mold them into our own. What I'm saying is that if we're not intentional about our passions and values, it's easy for us to look at society and believe the content it shares, but things aren't that simple. I know that the concept of *being present* is overstated in society, but the great thing about it is that if we're truly present, the superficial content society throws at us becomes senseless. Or rather, we're able to call out senseless content easily. When we're present, it means that we're coping with intentionality. But being present means that we are in the moment, right? Sort of, but yes, it means that there's no disconnect between our consciousness and its environment.

How Do You Build a Self-Care Practice?

Good question! I must remind you that when it comes to constructing these practices or determining which works, you must keep in mind that each of us differs from the next. Before you commit to a self-care practice, it's best to know which practices are important to you and especially to your overall health. For example, I personally believe that health is an important practice to include; in fact, I don't think that there's a self-care practice that exists without it. Now, health can be approached however broadly you prefer it to be. But, in terms of precision, it includes diet, fitness, sleep, and well-being. My point is that the practice you're including as a form of self-care is expansive. There isn't a particular limit to how many pillars (this word works, right?) each self-care practice should have. However, I know that the number of pillars often ranges between five and eight. For some clarification, let me break down the pillars that comprise my self-care practice:

- Health: As I explained, the pillar is expansive, and mine includes diet, fitness, sleep, and overall good health, all of which are included in my plan. Now, by including these, I'm making sure that each of them is being fed the right nutrients.

- Mental health: I believe that it's best for my overall mentality to keep this pillar separate from health. I do know that some people choose to bracket mental health and health together.

- Beauty: I admit that this one seems a bit superficial, but I assure you that's not the case. Beauty for me is split into morning and evening routines. Within this pillar, I like to allocate time for the salon or a massage.

- Success: Being successful is important to me. I have aspirations and goals, and reaching them is a priority for me. However, life gets extremely busy when there is no balance present.

- Relationships: It works best for me to grant relationships their own pillar; within this pillar, I prioritize communication and balance.

These five pillars make up my self-care practice; again, yours might have more pillars, and that's totally fine. Remember that this isn't about comparison, and the ultimate goal of the practice is to inform your mind of what is important and what should be sourced for your well-being. I previously mentioned that joy is cultivated through our self-care practices, and I've always thought of the self-care practice as being a nutrient to feed joy (we'll get into joy a bit later). However, the point is that when we're true to our needs (through self-care) we won't falter or mindlessly fill our mindsets with practices that offer us no sense of purpose. This is why intentionality is important; it prohibits emotions and actions that won't affect our well-being. When you're able to define those pillars of self-care for yourself, your boundaries will actively seek to ensure that your well-being is creating joy. I suppose it's another loop, but it makes sense, doesn't it?

I remember that when I began this process of constructing boundaries, people would ask me why I felt I needed them—I reckon they couldn't understand why the boundary demanded that much rule. For example, by not staying out late or not wanting to see certain people. To those who didn't comprehend this, it seemed as if I were investing my time in the wrong process. The truth is, no matter how hard you try to convince people of your reasons for wanting to improve—I think I might have used the phrase "personal growth" and a relative of mine just laughed at me—I've honestly given up on the narrative to convince them. I'm in a better place; I'm more joyful and open to new experiences and opportunities to improve myself. I suppose I'm more joyful.

Chapter 5:

Health and Boundaries

When you can't find someone to follow, you have to find a way to lead by example. –Roxane Gay

Let's begin with a simple question: What is health? To be frank with you, I do have a slight issue with the societal usage of the word, and for no reason other than consumerism. Health costs money, and it's quite a mental burden. The basic meaning of health is to be without sickness or illness, and really, that's what we strive for, isn't it? Health means that we're doing well, and when things are going well, they're not costing us any money. I don't mean to make this about money, but realistically, things are financially tough for most of us. This is why boundaries are great forces to employ in our lives. I'm not suggesting that by imposing the health boundary, you will be without sickness or illness; of course not. Unfortunate things have the habit of just happening. What I'm saying is that when the health boundary is imposed, there's no reason or not much reason to worry about those things. Consider this: A mindful diet paired with fitness and good sleep boosts our immune system and brain health. It's a great system.

Why is Health Important?

Well, ultimately, health is the center of life. It broadly encompasses everything we do, and without it, we're not able to function or reap any benefits. If you're in poor health, the chances of you achieving anything career-based are unlikely. The same goes for your mental health. If health is the center of our lives, it means that it's the core, or to be even more expressive, it's the heart of everything. Mental health requires optimal health to function; the same goes for our relationships. Here's another way of looking at it, most people use energy as a measurement of health. Think of energy as the fuse that links up everything—health is generally divided into four equal parts:

- Physical

- Mental

- Emotional

- Spiritual

Now, just for the sake of it, if you're wondering if these four categories of health could be a self-care practice, the answer is yes. You could simply snatch up these four constructs and set up boundaries for them. However, remember that everyone has their own preferences, and all you have to do is go with what works for you.

Diet

I always get weird about using the word diet—just to be clear, by "diet," I mean it literally. Actually, I also get weird about using the word "health", and to make matters complicated for myself, I'm using both of these words together. Society has definitely superficialized the presence of these two words. Note that I'm using both of these words for their basic definitions. A diet is your preference for meal choices, particularly meals that you habitually eat. Diets vary between people and cultures, and some of us seek a certain diet for health reasons and to lose weight. However, by diet, I am referring to the foods you're eating regardless of whether it's for health or simply out of habit.

A healthy diet serves to boost your body's immunity and protect it against possible diseases and illnesses. I mentioned that general advice for a diet is to eat the rainbow on your plate, and this simply means to include different nutritional foods. Nutrition is extremely important. I think that many misunderstand the concept of eating the rainbow because they don't take into account the nutritional value of foods. However, I'm not here to tell you what to eat or cut out of your diet. I don't think that it's anyone's place to do that, but I do advise you to always include something of nutritional value.

The last thing anyone wants is to cut out foods because someone else deems them unhealthy. Listen, if you're a chocolate person and love treats, you don't have to give them up. The golden word here is balance and how we maintain health and, honestly, also sanity—sugar withdrawals are real. Diets vary for us; if you're a person who eats without a specific reason (not in relation to a health diagnosis or for weight loss), then the only steps you need to follow to promote good health are mindfulness and balance. However, if you're a person who wants to lose weight, things are more tricky. You're going to have to reduce your current calorie intake, and this will affect the foods you're going to eat throughout the day.

Let's look at Morgan, who switched to a vegan diet and imposed a food boundary that prohibited him from eating out with certain groups of friends and family (non-vegans) due to their disregard to his food preferences. Morgan claimed that it was easier to skip food dates due to the choices available to him and admitted that inserting a boundary also prohibited him from overspending on foods that failed to satisfy him. Now, when it comes to food, it's also a good idea to cook for yourself when you're changing your diet. Many of us don't have the time (meal prep goes a long way) or are simply not intelligent cooks (hey, with time and practice, you can improve!). However, there is value in cooking for yourself; not only will you learn how to save money (and ingredients), but this process will teach you how to be more mindful and might even become a hobby for you. To reach even further, by introducing this action (to cook for yourself), it could establish itself as a form of relaxation.

But food is tricky, especially when it comes to family. Now, we know that change unfortunately affects those around us. Food tends to be the object that brings families together for occasions and holidays. Morgan explained that changing his diet made him realize that his family never respected it enough to cook or simply consider him. "They thought it was just a phase or something," he said, and he remembers that certain members would genuinely inquire about the diet. "I had to cater for myself at these events," he said, and though he didn't entirely mind, it took a toll on him. "I'd listen to them plan menus and whatnot and not think much about me; it got to the point where I'd shrug them off and be like, 'I'll sort myself out, don't worry.'" Morgan admits that this made him impose a boundary with his family too. "It wasn't personal, but, yeah, I needed them to know that my dietary needs are important. It took some time for them to catch up, but whenever we have these occasions, vegan options are included." Here are some tips for food and boundaries:

- Be clear with yourself and allow yourself permission to set this boundary, especially with your family. Remember that it's not personal, but it is necessary. Some people are known to ban certain body-related comments from the table or even diet talk. My friend explained that another issue was that he eventually began to hate explaining his reasons for choosing the diet. The goal is to be clear. Another thing that works is to plan out conversations in advance; this can help avoid negative remarks and possible miscommunication.

- Bring up your dietary preference during a neutral time. My friend states that whenever he was invited out to a restaurant or a get-together, he kindly reminded the person that he was a vegan and would have to check if there were suitable options for him. However, the same works for other diets. This is a great way to avoid unpleasant remarks, and it's also advisable to bring up your preference well in advance.

- Accept what you can control and what you cannot; there's no point in wasting energy on the matter. My friend advises that you clearly state your boundaries and let those around you know what your preferences are, but don't stick around to defend them meticulously. This will only end up tiring you, and it's likely that you'll fail to get your point across. You can't force people to understand or care enough to try.

- Move on when it's time to move on; again, there's no point in committing to a conversation that offers no room for comprehension. Disagreements, or rather, opinions, can cause intensity amongst people, so it's best to just get up and leave the room.

Fitness

The idea of being fit is expressively social, and the recent rise of fitness has become an impressive fascination among people. One can suggest that the pandemic has given rise to the cause, and ever since it ended (you know what I mean), online culture continues to grow in favor of fitness. I like online culture and encourage people to give YouTube a chance—it's always there (with a good connection) and it's free (even though you have to pay for that connection). I admit that the idea of being fit is odd and welcome to mind-toned six-packs. Listen, a six-pack doesn't define your fitness level. But fitness has become intensely linked to health; in fact, it's noted that one cannot be healthy if one doesn't exercise. Physical health is split into five components of fitness:

- Cardiorespiratory fitness is your body's ability to use oxygen and distribute it to the rest of your body.

- Musculoskeletal fitness comprises your muscle strength, endurance, and power.

- Flexibility (this is self-explanatory) is your joint's range of motion.

- Balance (again self-explanatory), simply your ability to maintain uprightness.

- Speed is your ability to move quickly.

As with the individuality of diets, the same goes for fitness. We each approach the action for varying reasons; some want to be fit and boost their health, some of us are interested in losing weight, and others are pursuing the action for health reasons. However, when fitness is paired with diet, they become an intense combination, and regardless of your reasons for pursuing either, they welcome incredible benefits. I must state that if you're pursuing a diet to lose weight and reduce your calorie intake, you must choose to follow an exercise regimen as well. The two practices must be paired if you want to succeed. There are many forms of exercise, but your preference is based on what works for you and your body. The challenging thing about introducing fitness to your life (if it's there already, I suppose the challenging thing about maintaining it) is finding time to see it through.

Identifying Your Values

Here are some questions to ask yourself:

- What motivates you to seek improvement in your fitness levels?

- What energizes you? This aims to help you understand which activities to remove from your daily life and which to pursue.

- What scares you about your current fitness level? Is it your health or the possibility of health issues arising?

- Who are you doing this for? The honest answer should be for yourself; often, we must investigate this question to properly determine those goals.

Here are some tips to help with your fitness boundaries:

- Be realistic with those boundaries; some of us may be suffering from certain health issues that prohibit the level and appearance of (fitness) success.

- Always communicate your boundaries; remember that establishing the importance of the boundary strengthens your attitude.

- Prepare yourself to enforce the boundary, make sure to set a specific time to practice your fitness, and do your best to respect it.

Sleep

Remember when I said that when you paired fitness and diet, you would reap success? Well, if you add sleep to the combination, you're going to reap even greater success. I think that when it comes to sleep, most of us have developed the attitude that sleep is something that can simply be caught up on. It can't, and whoever told you that (if it's coming from society, you should know better!) is lying to you. Sleep is a nutrient. A neuroscientist once elaborated on the prowess of sleep by saying that the body can manage without food and water for a notable amount of time; however, the body cannot function without sleep. I think of sleep as being the internal atmosphere within us; it's nutritious and complicated.

However, yes, the narrative spoken by society is that we don't need it if we're seeking to become successful. Another odd saying goes that sleep is meant only for death. These are senseless constructs. Sleep is directly infused with our brain health and improves its mood and performance. I know that you must have experienced sleeplessness the night before (if you're an insomniac or suffering from chronic fatigue, I feel for you) and found yourself unsuccessfully slugging through the day—this is how a lack of sleep affects your brain. Tasks that were considered easy or muscle memory become harder to enact; also, not getting enough sleep can risk the presence of diseases and disorders like strokes or obesity.

What Is Considered Good Sleep?

Sleep is complicated; it's divided into three properties: the first is the amount of sleep that you're getting; the second is the quality of this sleep (for example, it's important to have uninterrupted sleep cycles); and the third property is having a consistent sleep schedule. If each of these is working for rather than against each other, then you're sleeping toward success.

However, things become complicated for particular people who work night shifts or irregular hours. This is why the maintenance of a schedule and the force of a boundary is important. I think that when it comes to poor sleep people often shrug off its concern. Besides being a nutrient for the brain, sleep aids muscle and tissue repair as well. Your brain is still actively working during this phase and is known to be more awake than actual awakening.

I admit that on the surface, it seems odd that one must evoke boundaries to safeguard sleep, but I believe that the boundaries—though they're generally aimed at the public to obey—are first and foremost for ourselves. Some things possess the tendency to creep into sleep too easily, and often we just allow this because, after all, it's just sleep and something we can catch up on. However, that's not the case. When we're constantly reducing the amount of sleep we're getting, we're preparing our bodies for a crash or burnout. Also, you cause yourself to age at a rapid pace.

Respect your schedule, find a time, and stick to it. Go to bed at the same time each night and wake up at the same time as well. Now, it will be trickier, but with consistency, your body will allow this to become a habit. Also, when I say stick to your schedule, I mean weekends too. An actual time for bed and wakefulness is the boundary. To strengthen this boundary, the following can be used:

- Exercise every day. A little stretching goes a long way, but exercise promotes good health. However, it's recommended not to exercise close to your bedtime.

- Spending some time outdoors in natural and fresh sunlight does wonders for the mind. It's recommended to seek the sun upon wakefulness each morning, and I mean direct outdoor sunlight.

- Avoid caffeine and nicotine, though. I know it might be too difficult to give it up, so my advice is to reduce your intake. Caffeine is known to wear off around six to eight hours after consumption.

- Try to avoid naps, especially after mid-afternoon.

- Alcohol is another beverage you should consume in moderation if it's close to bedtime.

- Try to avoid large meals before bed too; they are known to affect your digestion, which will influence your sleep cycle.

- Limit the presence of devices before bed; you know that your phone is bad news. It's recommended to read or even meditate before sleep.

- Aim to create a healthy sleeping environment; cooler temperatures induce sleep faster; blacken your room; and don't forget to quiet your devices.

However, I'm aware that for some of us, sleep is an actual disorder that requires medication. If you find yourself still awake in bed, say, after twenty minutes, get up and go and do something else. You might go and read a book in a different room. Just don't stay in bed, and I know that I'm asking a lot; getting out of bed in the middle of the night is unpleasant. But if you stay, your brain will wake up even more and familiarize you with the purpose of your bed—that it's not for sleeping but for lying in. Remember that success is contingent on sleep; many people forget this, and the suggestion of sleeping only when you're dead is wrong. Work on your schedule and do your best to stick to it.

Mental Health

We live in a time where being depressed or feeling anxious are normal consequences of living in a technologically infused society. A part of me agrees with this opinion because it's true that the internet is a dangerous place for our overall mindsets and is often the cause of our painful dislike of society and people. A brief search on the internet will reveal that research has found intense correlations between social media and our deteriorating minds. I don't mean to come at society or technology, but I do believe that it's only proper to classify the dangerous role of these sources in our lives. Again, I think that the evolution of technology has been incredible to observe. However, I'm one of those people who doesn't entirely understand the need for more social media apps. But I get it, consumerism is important to capitalism.

Mental health is one of those societal concepts that doesn't receive enough conversation. Now, I'm not disregarding the many researchers and studies that are committed to sourcing causes and treatments for mental health disorders. Nor am I coming at anyone who is seriously battling a mental health disorder. If anything, you are in my prayers, and I sincerely wish you all the best with your recovery. Also, if you are going through something, I advise you to reach out to someone you trust and talk about what's happening with you. I also encourage you to seek help, though I am aware that seeking help is unfortunately costly. Whatever you're going through, I hope you make it through it.

Mental health is classified as our emotional, psychological, and social well-being. It comprises a series of disorders; the most famous ones are depression, anxiety, schizophrenia, and OCD. However, the actual list of these disorders is quite extensive, and treatment varies between them. Those of us who are battling mental health disorders are aware of how difficult life can be when there is no structure to our daily narratives. The power of a well-thought-out routine has risen in this regard. A routine is just another word for practice or ritual and falls into the category of self-care.

Mental health and boundaries are a good system; in fact, their symbiosis assures success. Now, you don't need to be diagnosed with a mental health disorder to use a boundary; many of our anxiety and depressive symptoms are undiagnosed. What I'm saying is that we know when we're feeling anxious or depressed without a doctor's sign-off, right? Of course, we do. The next step is to try to identify what your triggers are—try and locate what sort of situations affect these levels. Here are additional strategies:

- Focus on yourself and grant yourself this permission, because I know that it can be unsettling and uncomfortable to constantly think about your feelings in relation to other people. I've been in situations where I complicated my boundaries by adapting them to the other person's needs; this sabotaged my mental health. For example, if I go to a certain place, I once had a horrible experience in the cinema, and whenever I'm there, especially if the cinema is modestly filled, I begin to panic. I tried going with friends, but it ended up costing me too much stress. So, I don't go to the cinema for the sake of my anxiety. I've learned that when it comes to the health of boundaries and their maintenance, they only work when self-respect and self-love are initiated by the self.

- Practice self-awareness—actually, I'm one of those people who prefers listening to their gut and am always encouraging people to work on their gut. When self-awareness is evoked, we're able to comprehend what safety and presence mean in relation to ourselves and our circumstances.

- Understand your limitations. Reflection is key, okay. Again, I know that it might be uncomfortable to sit and reflect on your emotions, but it's necessary for your well-being. When we're reflecting on our day or situations, we're going to learn what our physical, emotional, and mental needs are. There is an exercise that requires you to draw a circle on a page. Inside the circle, you must write down everything you need to feel safe. By safety, I mean what you need to feel seen by others, respected, heard, and supported. On the outside of this, write down anything that conflicts with these emotions. This can help you understand triggers and how to remove yourself from situations that can cause them.

- Always be consistent. I mean, things will get difficult, but that's no excuse for you to stretch them or adapt them to the needs of those around you. If you feel that your boundaries are being threatened, I advise you to communicate these feelings with the people threatening them. I know that talking about the boundary or how you might feel is wrong and scary, but the truth is it makes me nervous too. However, always begin the conversation with "I feel." It goes a long way.

- Always be direct and clear, and keep your words simple. I have a cousin who naturally overexplains everything because she feels no one understands her. Words are very important when we're talking about our mental health and its boundaries. There isn't a right or wrong way of speaking; some of us might prefer a more assertive tone, while others prefer a more emotionally driven one. Go with what works for you, but remember to be kind.

Preserving Personal Growth

Sometimes, when we're working on ourselves and ultimately seeking personal growth, we forget about happiness, or rather, the placement of happiness in our lives. I remember that when I began this process of change and boundaries, the sensation of happiness slipped away from me, and I convinced myself that this was okay. Once I had figured things out and settled into my new position as a person, happiness would locate me again. It's all really backward; that's not how happiness should work for anyone. Though, really, happiness has always felt a bit odd for me, especially when it's compared to joy. Happiness is defined as a state, as something we enter, and this has always thrown me off because it feels permanent. I'm well aware of the notion that nothing in life is permanent or guaranteed, but emotions are different, or at least they should be. Joy is different, defined as an emotion evoked by our well-being. To me, joy feels as if it's always been saturated within me, regardless of what I'm going through, whereas happiness comes and goes depending on my mood.

I brought up the difference between the two states with friends, and they found themselves opinionatively split. I don't think happiness is a legit enough emotion, or rather, I don't think it's sustainable. The more I consider its presence, the more I'm reminded of the times I felt happy. I read somewhere philosophically that happiness can only be identified after we experience a moment that renders the sensation. You'll only know that you were happy after it happened, so in recollection only. Apparently, no one knows that they're happy in the moment. Joy is different; it's lodged within our well-being and if we're always in balance, meaning if joy receives its wonderful nutrients, it's always there.

Another difference between the two sensations is that happiness is the result of an experience, while joy is not. This means that you can be joyful in the presence of happiness or an experience. It's just dependent on the state of your well-being. I've been thinking a lot about personal growth—after all, it's why I constructed these boundaries. I know that each of us wants success, and success is defined by our personality and not society, and often our mental states are disregarded for the idea of the bigger picture. Honestly, during my transition to change, there were moments I felt depressed. We spoke about how change affects the lives of those around us, but it also affects us. I lost friendships and missed out on socialization. I think the worst thing about the socialization part was the memories those people made without me. But change forced me to address my financial state and my romance as well.

As wonderful as the overall benefits are, they were uncomfortable. I remember feeling depressed here and there. I suppose when you're putting your life in perspective, unfortunately, reality has to hit you hard. Happiness wasn't present, and I was conscious of it. I think the internet presents a fake image of people getting their lives in order, and I'm writing this to you from a place of care—it's difficult, I know. But I didn't know that happiness wasn't an actual state, and maybe you didn't know this as well. It's why I'm telling you to continue feeding your well-being with nutrients (self-care) because it will take care of you. It's lodged within you, simply waiting to flow again.

Society speaks a lot about self-care and its importance, but I don't think I've ever seen them associate self-care with joy. Looking back at how uncomfortable I was then, I wish someone had told me that the bigger picture wasn't happiness at the end of the tunnel. A depressed me faltered when it came to my boundaries. I want to be clear, practicing self-care and joy won't prohibit your mental health disorder (if you have one), but I know that a good mindset helps and can promote growth. However, here are additional steps to help you cultivate joy in your life:

- Focus on your self-care practice. The more time you spend focusing on your well-being the stronger the sensation of joy becomes within you. Remember that intentionality is key to our ultimate success and personal growth.

- Be kind. I know that it's the general rule (and we will get into this in another chapter), but by kindness, I simply mean that you must reduce negativity, or rather, negative self-talk. Once we're able to reduce the limit of negative self-talk within us, our outlook on life becomes more positive.

- Enjoy yourself. Building boundaries is an arduous process, and like I said, it affects your mental capacity. The trick is to begin slowly and to always be intentional about the experiences you're having. Self-care is about compiling all the things we find important about ourselves and related to ourselves into a healthy mindset.

- Seek out support. I think that it's great to construct a good and healthy support system, and since our boundaries reduce friendships for us, know that these are the people who choose to stick it out with you. Some people have this narrative that it's them against the world. It's not and shouldn't be; people are important.

- Practice gratitude. Sometimes we get drawn to negative feelings, and the slightest thing can set us off into a bad mood and mindset. I think that the way we begin each day should be of extreme importance. I used to have this habit of checking my emails and hoping that there wasn't a bad one from a client or something. In the morning, I try to meditate: It's difficult, and I'm only able to do it for about five minutes before I begin my morning routine.

- Be mindful. Intentionality and mindfulness are the same practice; it's the action of being aware of our presence in relation to ourselves and the environment.

Remember, this is naturally an uncomfortable process; take your time and be joyful.

Chapter 6:

Boundaries: Managing Your Success and Finances

It's the possibility of having a dream come true that makes life interesting.
—Paulo Coelho

Honestly, I hate talking about success; it feels too fluid, and in the back of my head, I'm certain I'm offending the next person. It's also a difficult topic to talk about; realistically, all of us won't be successful—according to the hierarchy system of society. Another issue is that success is always only associated with careers, and that welcomes another issue because the majority of us are working jobs and not careers. Success means accomplishing a goal that you set for yourself. That sounds rather minor and ordinary, doesn't it?

What Are Money Boundaries?

Money boundaries or financial boundaries refer to your personal wealth and the unhealthy tendency you have to provide friends and family with funds that are either never returned to you or hinder your own financial growth by placing you in debt. However, money boundaries also refer to the unhealthy spending habits you might have. Money boundaries are therefore split into two categories: for yourself and for others. Yes, it's possible to experience both categories:

- For yourself: This refers to your spending habits or failure to save money.

- For others: This refers to your availability to provide funds to friends and family at the expense of your own well-being.

Why Are Money Boundaries Important?

Ultimately, by abiding by the rules of money boundaries, you're safeguarding your future and prioritizing your needs. We tend to find ourselves constantly wanting things due to societal pressure and poor mental health issues. But when we're able to safeguard our spending habits, we're able to think (and spend) beyond our current means. The truth is, people can overwhelm your budget, and at the start, it may not seem detrimental to your budget or finances. But when we're not strict about our finances, people will begin to take advantage. Here are some tips:

- Understand what your finances are; the salary at the end of the month is not the actual amount of money you're going to have after deductions. For example, the rent, water and electricity bills, food bills, car (if you have one), insurance, and possibly the bills of a child.

- Be honest with what your needs are; this is where you'll have to sit and draw up a list of needs and wants. We often say we want a car, a home, or a luxury vacation, but never treat these things as goals. When we establish these sorts of wants as goals, we're able to improve our mindsets and influence our financial goals.

- Work on your budget; we all need one, and oftentimes they fail because our priorities and needs aren't clear.

How Do You Set Financial Boundaries for Yourself?

You're going to require some critical thinking skills to help you set up these boundaries. Most of the time, the reason we overspend or are careless about our spending habits is due to mental health pressure and societal pressure. Here's what to do:

1. Be clear about your financial goals: For example, if you plan to retire at a specific age or want to buy a house, you're going to need to draw up a financial plan to figure out how to move toward these goals. A financial adviser can be sourced.

2. Create a budget: The budget should revolve around your current income; you must be realistic about your needs and wants. There are a variety of budgeting methods to follow, so pick one that will best suit your lifestyle.

3. Prioritize your goals: Most of the time, our goals are influenced by wealth. For example, if your goal is to purchase a car or home, your spending habits (and budget) should revolve around the goal.

4. Be strict about lending money: You must be clear with those around you. One of the most common rules people have is to never borrow money from family or friends. Some people won't lend money and simply give whatever they can spare from their budget.

5. Be strict about gifting: Only if your budget allows for it, you could try to save a specific amount of money each

month for circumstances that require lending money or purchasing gifts.

6. Advocate for yourself: Money is a difficult conversation to have with people, especially when neither of you is earning compatible salaries. For example, if your friends suggest dinner and someone opts for an expensive restaurant, speak up and suggest a more affordable one instead of writing off the expense on a credit card or feeling uncomfortable.

7. Don't cover shared expenses: Sometimes we find ourselves in a situation where the bill is dealt with as a joint expense as opposed to an individual expense, and we find ourselves paying more. Speak up and be clear that you're only covering your expenses.

8. Be mindful of family events: The holidays and birthdays can be stressful if you're not mindful of how much your budget can cover. Remember that the main focus is your goals (home, car, retirement) and that gifts and family trips shouldn't affect these goals. Be upfront with your family about your budget and how much you're willing to spend; this way, all parties are aware and given the option to change plans before they are permanently set.

9. Communicate clearly: Money will always be tricky to discuss with people; you don't have to be specific about your exact earnings (in fact, never share this with people). Simply share your goals, and if you can't attend certain events, let them know that your budget prohibits you.

10. Be prepared for pushback: People will hold grudges if you stop lending them money or are constantly advocating for more affordable options. If necessary,

it's okay to take a step back from people who don't respect your need for boundaries.

How to Set Financial Boundaries for Others?

Remember that to set these boundaries, we must first be clear and upfront with ourselves:

1. Always respect your budget. We previously discussed deductions from salary and how the better option might be a gift (if the budget is respected and money is saved).

2. Have a clear and direct conversation with people and express your goals to them so that they can understand why you can't help them financially.

3. Accept that you're going to upset people; changing your behavior, especially prioritizing yourself, will cause resentment from others. It's okay to take some space away from them.

4. Offer them non-financial support; they may not want this, but it can positively help them through the mental health issues impacting their finances.

5. Be sensitive about loaning money; be honest and sincere about your inability to lend money. For example, "As much as I'd love to help, I'm not in the position to loan you money."

6. Advocate for the budget-friendly option even if you can afford it; this is about establishing boundaries with those around you.

7. Set up a payment date with those you've loaned money to; for example, if you covered a friend's meal, kindly

ask your friend to transfer the money they owe you before leaving.

8. Remember that the bill should always be split individually and not equally—pay only what you are willing to spend on yourself.

Do We All Need Money Boundaries?

Yes, we all should have money boundaries and shouldn't feel guilty about imposing them on those around us. Money boundaries are ideally about prioritization, helping you plan for retirement while considering what your values and needs are as a person. Money boundaries aren't about being strict or cheap, but simply choosing to respect the need for a budget and the future. However, our finances become pressured when we find ourselves consistently providing money to those around us at a disadvantage.

Strengthening Your Mindset

I think that the great thing about our minds is our ability to learn, and yes, learning gets a bad rep due to a variety of reasons. However, I don't think society is clear enough about learning or upskilling traits and characteristics. Something that took me a while to realize about the working world is how much growth is needed to succeed.

Enhance Your Growth Mindset

The mindset is defined as an established set of attitudes located within each person; this implies that these attitudes are based on our individuality. However, the mindset is split into two basic sections that are influential toward a person's perception of themselves and their abilities. The mindsets are:

- Fixed mindset

- Growth mindset

Ideally, one is better than the other. Those with a growth mindset view (based on those established set attitudes) have intelligence, abilities, and talents that are learnable and able to improve with effort and determination. However, those possessing a fixed mindset view intelligence, abilities, and talents as static and unchangeable elements. You see where this is going, right? I'm sure, based on the example of my friend and her promotion, she'd be considered to possess a growth mindset. Another example is, say that you're beginning a business and you require some basic financial skills to be able to construct budgets and statements:

- A fixed mindset would likely doubt their ability, presenting them with reasons like always being bad at math or unable to understand the layout of statements. Whatever the reasons, the mindset has now lodged itself in doubt and disbelief about success.

- A growth mindset would accept the requirements needed; they would acknowledge the skills they're lacking and immediately begin to learn and find practices to improve their skills.

Doubt is definitely one of the major aggressors in this regard; once it's present, it's difficult to push aside. But this is why we have boundaries. If you're serious about improving your mindset—and know that the growth mindset extends beyond that of just business and can improve your perception of life— the next step would be to switch some bad habits around and carve out genuine time for improvement. Let's look at my own life quickly. During the week, I have some free time where I choose to sit and watch TV or read a book or something. I could introduce growth as a pillar of self-care and enclose it with a boundary. I could tell myself that for the next three months, this boundary is going to help me commit to learning these skills.

Regardless of your reasons for seeking to improve your mindset, growth should always be your aim. People with a growth mindset ultimately believe that they are able to control their lives, while those with a fixed mindset believe things are out of their control. Now, it doesn't help that society pesters that *what will be will be* or *it is what it is*; these sorts of remarks offer no legitimate substance, and you shouldn't allow them status. You shouldn't, because we're in the business of boundaries over here, and the mere existence of a boundary working efficiently dissuades that senseless chatter. Healthy boundaries prove that things can be controlled because they can be changed. Here's how to improve your mindset toward growth:

- Believe that effort makes the difference, and this is a crucial step. Change requires effort and determination. Ultimately, you're going to have to believe in yourself.

- Be open to learning new skills; this is how we improve, and why we need to believe that effort makes all the difference. Learning anything is difficult; remember that as you improve, things will get simpler.

- Change your outlook on failure; it doesn't mean that you've failed. If anything, it's a lesson teaching you how to improve your skills. It's also a time for critical reflection and allows you to reappraise the situation from a different viewpoint.

Enhance Your Emotional Intelligence

Emotions are tricky, and I don't think I've ever seen society insert the narrative that we should gain intelligence in order to comprehend their power and influence. The basic meaning of emotional intelligence is the brain's ability to use, understand, utilize, and gain reason through the process of emotions. It's suggested that those of us who possess emotional intelligence possess the ability to not only understand their own emotions but also the emotions of those around them. So, why is emotional intelligence important? The short answer is that modernism allows us to use emotions as fuel, and currently, the world feels like an emotional state. When it comes to self-love, we're always encouraged to figure ourselves and our emotions out in order to comprehend what it is that we need. Note that we will get into emotions in the next chapter. However, another good way to improve upon your emotional intelligence is to:

- Pay attention to your emotions; no one is in a better place to comprehend these feelings.

- Manage your emotions by taking a step back and reflecting on what you're feeling or what happened.

- Try to always listen to others; our opinions are too quick to dismiss others.

Work on Your Mental Toughness

Resilience goes a long way, and it's a skill that can successfully equip you for the future. It's claimed that those with remarkable resilience or mental toughness view challenges as opportunities—this is great, right? Well, these people feel that they have significant control over their lives and destiny; in short, they have great motivation skills. Here's how to improve this skill:

- Believe in yourself and reduce the negative self-talk.

- Always try. I know that it's difficult, especially when things become hard, but the consistency of trying is what will get you through the day and toward the future.

- Care for yourself. I think that many of us forget about this, and when we're establishing boundaries, we need to practice physical and emotional care.

- Always look toward the future, and I encourage you to look for opportunities that can boost growth.

Boundaries in the Workplace

Benefits of workplace boundaries:

- Your productivity levels are going to increase, and this is going to positively affect your career and goals.

- Your work-stress levels will reduce, allowing you to accomplish more and reducing the possibility of mental health issues.

- You'll be consistent with your workload, which means that as a professional, you're going to be reliable and able to build a good relationship with your colleagues as trustworthy.

- The risk of enduring burnout will decrease significantly.

- You're ultimately going to set good examples for those around you and hopefully inspire them to not only respect your boundaries and yourself but have them follow in your footsteps.

Tips on Maintaining Workplace Boundaries

1. Set priorities: This works in both your personal and professional lives; be clear and direct. The goal is to identify the skills you need for these priorities, which will ultimately improve yourself.

2. Delegate tasks: The goal isn't about accomplishing it all in one day or being that person who overexerts and does everything themselves. This will lead to burnout and mental stress, and neither of these symptoms is needed for your well-being. So be specific and open to sharing the responsibility of the task. You may be pressured to over-excel at work, but taking on too much work will lead to burnout and failure.

3. Understand your workload: On the surface, things look manageable; in your head, you may be able to plan out things successfully; however, in person, you may find yourself failing. Be realistic about your goals and understand how much you can manage.

4. Take time off: Rest will improve your ability to achieve your goals; don't fear it or let it undermine your self-worth. Feeling sick is a great sign that you've been working too much, so if you need the afternoon or morning off, don't beat yourself up about it. You are allowed sick days.

5. Communicate openly with those around you; if you feel overwhelmed or depressed, share these feelings with

the people in your life. The last thing you want is to suffer from any form of breakdown at work.

6. Ask for advice; don't overcomplicate the concept that you need to know everything to climb the career ladder. Most people appreciate being approached to help. This shows people that you are interested in learning and expanding your knowledge.

7. Set limits; you shouldn't be overworking yourself or spending after-work hours finishing work you are not being paid for. Know and respect your limits; also, taking work home with you when you have family or relationships is tricky to manage. The last thing you want is to let the other person feel useless or unimportant; setting boundaries protects these forms of relationships.

8. Following a schedule; most people struggle with this one, but it helps us meet both our professional and personal goals without having either one aggressively impede the other.

9. Be honest; if you're struggling to be open about it, workplace stress has the habit of following you home and will negatively affect your relationship. If you are no longer happy with your job or colleagues, boundaries need to be established to protect everything important to you. You should visit the HR department for further assistance.

10. Respect your colleagues; you don't have to like them or be friends with them. However, be realistic; you have to spend time with them daily, so be mindful and professional.

11. Be clear about your job responsibilities; we tend to confuse and overexert our capabilities. It's best to

discuss your responsibilities with your supervisor so that you're clear on what your actual duties are within the company.

12. Prepare for confrontations; not everyone is meant to get along, and though we all aim to be professionals, we might struggle with proper communication in the workplace. If issues arise with your colleague, be professional and visit the HR department.

13. Practice saying "no." This might be the most common advice to practice, but it's best to make peace with declining invitations or requests.

Raise Your Motivation

Motivation requires willpower, and willpower is defined as your ability to control yourself and ultimately your mindset. When our willpower is strengthened, difficulties become easier to manage. Also, possessing perseverance as a characteristic can be beneficial. The thing is, we get bored sometimes or even tired when we're constantly doing the same thing repeatedly. But willpower is the type of characteristic that forces us to continue. For example, when we're distracted, a lack of willpower will convince us to give up. Maybe you're trying to lose weight and are struggling to keep away from snacks (sounds like a boundary need, right?). By introducing a distraction, you're shifting your mind from the snack. So, with willpower, you could opt to pick up a healthier snack or even go for a walk.

Success requires realism. Motivation to become a millionaire is great and doable, I suppose, but it's not realistic or sustainable. My personal relationship with success sometimes feels complicated and mostly uneventful when things seem to go against me. Losing motivation is a normal sensation for us, and honestly, it's something that affects me from time to time. For a long time, I've been wondering about how to make my motivation to climb the career ladder and achieve an impressive and sustainable savings account. Dreams can only get us that far, right? I think that part of the problem is that we lose a sense of meaning, or the reality of it slips into more superficial ideals.

It's okay to sometimes lose faith in the process or the journey you began. We're humans (not that I think it's a good excuse), but we live in a space of time that constantly moves us from A to C without including B. When your motivation is lacking, here's what to do:

- Challenge yourself. A collection of goals can seem overwhelming and even boring, so I created a new challenge. It doesn't have to be a monumental endeavor; in fact, the smaller the better. It's like we're trying to rebuild the habit of accomplishing a goal. Challenges keep the brain interested; they improve your self-esteem, and that negative voice in your head will morph into something more positive. Also, the easier the challenge, the more difficult it will become. By constantly accomplishing your goals, you're going to crave mightier ones, and sooner rather than later, you'll be back where you began.

- Maintain your curiosity; remember that curious minds inform the brain's view of success and growth. Curiosity will encourage you to seek new experiences and knowledge, and we know that when we improve our skills, we're improving our future. I'm a reader, so I prefer reading across subjects.

- Understand your control; yes, this is about being intentional about the things happening to you. Sometimes I become frustrated when a friend says this or that is out of their control. Though this statement has truth, it's not entirely true, and the statement shouldn't be used as a reason for why you failed. Control is about knowing that you possess real influence over your life.

- Competition is okay but keep it healthy. I think that when we're too competitive, we lose track of our self-worth and that of others. Each of us wants to accomplish something and, more importantly, wants to win. Competition allows for comparison, and as with the example above, this isn't good. These days, I look at other people and try to reflect on my own life, not necessarily to compare but to understand my goals.

The trick is to keep things clear and practical with yourself. Sometimes the emotions of other people negatively creep into our lives, but this is okay; as I said, it offers room for reflection. Keep in mind that success is about accomplishing goals, regardless of how small or insincere they may appear to you. Sometimes we lose track of our goals, especially when we notice other people are achieving theirs easily or even overnight. We know that this isn't true; things take time, and time requires hard work to see it through. When our mindset and overall well-being are in balance, a boundary can do well to enforce our motivation.

Chapter 7:

Boundaries within

Relationships

Just because your version of normal isn't the same as someone else's version doesn't mean that there's anything wrong with you. —John Boyne

I think that of all possible things to create boundaries for, relationships might be the most complex one, and due to many reasons, of course. Though one of the main reasons is that this boundary directly deals with people, our previous ones were related to the self and simply conditioned toward other people. However, relationships are contingent on the presence of other people, and if we're not specific about the people we allow to enter our lives, we're risking our sanity and health. People are complicated, and though this isn't a reason to do away with them, it is enough to consider whether or not their intentions are good or bad. However, I must admit that I view relationship boundaries in two categories, one is about our relationship with people, and the other is about our relationship with constructs or establishments. However, when relationships necessitate boundaries, it's usually due to toxicity.

Signs That Toxicity May Be Present in Your Relationship	
Support	There's a lack of support present within a relationship, and you've noticed more negative experiences within this relationship.

Signs That Toxicity May Be Present in Your Relationship	
	This affects us poorly because when there's a lack of support present, we ultimately feel as if the needs of others are more important than our own and that we aren't valued.
Communication	There's tension in communication with certain people, which means that there's more sarcasm, criticism, and contemptuous commentary taking place.
Envy and Jealousy	There may be inconsistent feelings of envy and jealousy that you experience in certain situations or with people. Though these are normal feelings, they can lead to intense negative experiences and hinder personal growth.
Control	Do you have a partner, friend, or relative who's constantly suspicious of your whereabouts and irritated by your response time or choices?
Resentment	Toxicity begins to fester when we hold grudges and dismiss healthy communication with people, and this is due to feeling unsafe during conversation.
Dishonesty	If you've been lying about your whereabouts or about the people you were with in fear of how your partner (or another person) may

Signs That Toxicity May Be Present in Your Relationship

	react to the truth, it's a sign of a toxic relationship that can evolve into abuse.
Disrespect	We tend to feel this way when a person constantly breaks a promise, forgets an important thing, or is simply always late. It makes us feel as if we're not important or not being heard.
Finance	Finances, especially shared finances, can cause tension within any relationship and become problematic when the other person doesn't have a budget, savings, or share equal responsibility.
Stress	Stress is a constant figure in our lives and most of the time manageable, but when we feel constantly on the edge due to the presence of other people, this sort of stress affects you physically and mentally and ultimately feels exhausting.
Needs	This is when you're disregarding your needs for the other person; it becomes so damaging that you end up going against your desires, wishes, and comfort level.
Lost Relationships	Lost relationships are a result when you've consciously chosen to avoid and prohibit the

Signs That Toxicity May Be Present in Your Relationship	
	possibility of conflict.
Lack of self-care	Due to stress, you're too fatigued to take care of yourself and find that you've withdrawn from society, neglected your health, and may have even sacrificed your free time at the expense of other people.
Hopefulness	This is brought on by denial and the delusional belief that if you stay in a relationship, things will change. Most of the time, you end up believing that you are the one who has to change yourself or actions to salvage the relationship. This isn't how change works.
Eggshells	This is when worry forces you to watch yourself, especially your actions in the relationship, so that you don't cause any issues.

Can You Fix a Toxic Relationship?

Yes, you can, but it ultimately depends on all parties involved in the relationship. There is no point in fixing yourself for the relationship if your partner isn't doing the same. The relationship will remain unhealthy, and change won't occur. However, if both parties aren't unanimous about the relationship, you're likely going to have to address the need for boundaries. Remember that toxicity is one of the main culprits affecting the health of our boundaries. If we're setting boundaries in a toxic environment, we're setting ourselves up for failure. Most of the time, we find ourselves in toxic relationships due to a lack of support. If you're in a committed relationship with someone and are going to set boundaries, be mindful of your partner and how they may feel about the boundaries. This isn't to say that the boundary shouldn't be set, but that a lack of healthy communication can create a toxic misunderstanding.

The last thing you want to do is let your partner or anyone else feel as if they are the reason you're setting boundaries, so be mindful and clear about the need for boundaries. If you've found that your relationship has tilted into toxicity, here are some tips to help you repair communication:

1. Don't dwell on the past; this is about repairing the relationship and preparing it for your boundaries. Don't make the other person feel as if it is their fault for the input of boundaries. Remember that you're setting boundaries for your wellbeing.

2. Be compassionate; this person may likely feel as if it's their fault or as if they directly influence the negativity within the relationship. Boundaries are specific to you; however, be mindful of the other person and what they may be feeling.

3. Seek therapy if your communication skills aren't effective. A therapist can help you communicate and establish the individual need for establishing boundaries.

4. Be accountable for your actions, especially your language, and be mindful of your non-verbal communication.

5. Ultimately, toxicity requires individual healing, so be open to allowing the other person room to heal and adapt to the change occurring within the relationship.

Why Do We Need Boundaries in Our Relationships?

Because no person is the same and therefore won't respect your needs or mental health in the same way. It's easy to take advantage of; most of the time, we find ourselves experiencing life on autopilot and unaware of the pain and toxicity we find ourselves in. Relationship boundaries, especially between a couple, are temperamental; not only do they serve to define ownership and responsibility, but they are ultimately informed by trust and respect. Most people believe that the most common boundary-related issues with relationships are romantic ones. I don't agree with this and associate this viewpoint with the narrative the media releases—it's always without context. Now, we previously spoke of emotional intelligence and the concept of being mindful or attuned to your emotions and those of others. I believe that each person should strive to understand their emotions. I don't think that everyone will successfully achieve emotional intelligence; however, I still believe that it makes a ton of difference to the lives of other people. I know what this might sound like— shouldn't the people we choose to keep in our lives be emotionally intelligent?

Romance

This brings me to romantic relationships; we each want an emotionally mature partner because emotions are difficult and confusing. So, here's the question, do you stick it out if your partner isn't interested in gaining a form of emotional intelligence? In romantic relationships, the usage of time, space, body, and energy are at the forefront of the "tools" needed to sustain the connection. Each of these "tools" should have a boundary encased around it. If you're not comfortable sharing your space, time, body, and energy with a person, you shouldn't be in that relationship. Here's another thing, those four "tools" should be considered symbiotic, meaning that if three out of four work for you, the one that doesn't is the tiebreaker that moves you along.

If you're going to stick it out, you're going to be crossing your boundaries and setting yourself up for emotional failure. A healthy romantic relationship comprises these four "tools," each abiding by the rule of the boundary. Honestly, in romance, you want a partner who will respect these boundaries without you having to constantly enforce them. Additionally, romantic boundaries extend physically as well. If you're at your significant other's home and you're not comfortable staying over, a healthy boundary could be establishing a set time to go home. Another boundary could be related to the frequency of your texts or when the cutoff time for replies will end. But these boundaries extend to how often you see this person, what sort of dates you're going to have, and even establishing sexual expectations. Communication is key to every relationship, so talk to this significant person.

Family

Families can be complicated and toxic, and I find that many of us are drawn to constructing boundaries because our family life is simply too much. However, I believe that families are the last to know about boundaries and probably the most confused about why you had to establish one. There are many reasons for the family boundary; some of these reasons are fueled with more intensity, and some of us might have come from physically abusive families. In this regard, I think distance pairs well with the boundary. The reason why family boundaries are so complicated is due to their presence. If your family is simply toxic or selfish, distance isn't always the best option; therefore, you must work on limiting your time with them.

Perhaps you have had experience with a relative who calls you multiple times a day, or maybe their opinions are too aggressive and make you feel uncomfortable. Listen, it's okay to tell these people how you feel in these situations. If they're open to change and compromise, time can help you figure things out. Though it's likely that they won't understand during this period, I encourage you to evoke some distance while both parties are aiming to figure things out. Another issue with the family boundary is that we tend to be a bit too soft, meaning that we easily excuse their lack of comprehension and end up disregarding our feelings. Families can, unfortunately, horribly dictate your time and presence in their lives.

We establish this boundary because we're committing to our overall well-being. Healing from family-related toxicity requires time and patience, and honestly, this is your time to rebuild the image you hold of yourself. There's no point in forcing people or relatives to comprehend, and those that don't simply can't respect the boundary—remember that this is why you established the boundary; if someone can't respect it, there's no need for their presence in your life. However, distance is often the best form of boundary to evoke with family.

Boundary Violations in Romantic Relationships

Oftentimes, we forget that boundaries are needed in romantic relationships or that, as long-term partners, we often overstep them. Here are some boundaries and limits to be mindful of within your relationship:

- When you say "yes" instead of "no" to your partner, you usually do this to avoid conflict; this also suggests that we've entered into a codependent relationship that prioritizes the needs and emotions of the other person over our own and the state of the relationship.

- When we say "no" when the right answer is "yes," we tend to do this to either punish or be spiteful toward the other person. This means that the relationship has generated its fair share of resentment and that healthy communication is no longer available.

- Relying on the silent treatment; remember that regardless of how long you've been a couple, your partner isn't capable of reading your mind.

- Being passive-aggressive throughout the relationship to gain control.

Healthy Boundaries to Enhance Your Relationship

Here are some tips to help you maintain the health of your relationship:

- Make sure you're communicating as honestly and directly as possible. We discussed communication in Chapter 3. Remember that your partner will never develop the ability to read your mind, so be open about your feelings in a respectful way.

- Always ask your partner about their feelings; don't guess or claim to know what they are feeling. Remember, this isn't about the past; keep the conversation current and don't bring up past instances.

- Don't avoid the conversation; if your partner feels they want to share and you don't feel ready, practice active listening and be mindful of your non-verbal language. After you effectively communicate with your partner (remember to reflect and repeat), ask for time before you respond. This shouldn't serve as avoidance and shouldn't be dragged out; always aim to respond effectively.

- Take responsibility for your actions; don't avoid blame by pointing the finger at your partner. Be respectful and intentional; remember that you both want to fix the relationship and the issue occurring.

Non-Negotiable Boundaries in Romantic Relationships

Any form of toxicity or codependency in a relationship is unhealthy; however, there are additional types of issues that shouldn't be present in the relationship. If behaviors within the relationship are built on physical, emotional, or sexually abusive tendencies, it is time to leave the relationship and find a safe space. Here are some non-negotiable boundaries to be mindful of:

- Any form of physical abuse shouldn't be present in your relationship. For example, if you're being hit, pushed, shoved, or held down against your will, this is a sign of abuse.

- If you want to leave and the exit is purposely being blocked by the other person, this is a sign of abuse.

- If feelings of extreme jealousy are present.

- If the other person is constantly in need of knowing your whereabouts throughout the day.

- If you're constantly being checked on throughout the day and questioned about the people you're with.

- If you're isolated from your friends and family.

- If the person in the relationship constantly directs degrading and shameful comments at you.

- Any form of controlling behaviors.

- Sexual violence, for example, rape, coercion, pressure, or marital rape.

- If any form of intimidation or threat is being used.

Relationships with Constructs

The following four boundaries are considered elemental or focused on internal constructs of the mind:

Physical Boundaries

This form of boundary means all things physical and about the body, privacy, and personal space. Physical boundaries are known to take effect in relationships, and common examples could be kissing in public or PDA. Some of us are fine with displaying our relationships and intimacy in public spaces. However, some are uncomfortable with this sort of behavior. If you are this person, I suggest that you talk to your partner. Personal space can relate to being out with strangers at a grocery store or something. Personal boundaries are the kind of boundaries that require specific communication because they're usually in conversation with another person, like in a romantic relationship, for example. Jane and Paul are in a relationship, but Paul would never hold Jane's hand in public, and when she confronted him about it, he dismissed it and said that he didn't like physical touch in public spaces. Jane's friends called this a red flag; obviously, if he didn't want to showcase the relationship in public, it meant that he didn't want people to know about them, especially other women. Jane and Paul broke up, and though we can discuss the superficiality of the breakup, the point is that we each have preferences. Also, not every preference—for example, Paul's dismal PDA—requires a deep emotional breakdown.

Communication is key to healthy boundaries and their overall maintenance. Things might look and sound a certain way, but only conversation can truly offer a better comprehension of the situation. Also, honesty goes a long way. Another thing that creeps into physical boundaries is mental health disorders, particularly anxiety. Some of us suffering from anxiety avoid certain spaces. However, whatever your reason, remember to communicate it with those around you.

Emotional Boundaries

A great way to fully explore emotions is through reflection, whether it's by journaling or meditation. Our emotional boundaries must be thriving alongside health. The thing about emotions is that if we're not mature enough to deal with them, they end up affecting those around us. Emotional maturity is necessary when we're trying to better ourselves and our overall well-being. Emotional maturity means that you can manage your emotions. I know that this might sound daunting, but it is true that emotions often need to be managed. Here are some tips to help you:

- Take a minute to check in with yourself and reflect on whatever you're feeling.

- Accept all of your emotions, even if they are bad and unfair.

- Always jot down your thoughts; not only is this a great way to reflect, but we're also actualizing the emotions.

- Always breathe; we tend to forget that we need to at times.

Sexual Boundaries

This is linked with romance and also physical forms of boundaries. Sexual boundaries are complicated and somewhat uncomfortable to discuss. The aim is to begin the conversation at the start of the relationship; this way, things are clear and there's less pressure to uphold certain preferences. Sexual boundaries include but are not limited to,

- Sexual comments

- Unwanted sexual touch

- Monogamy

- Sexual acts

Healthy sexual boundaries will provide mutual agreement, consent, and understanding of your partner's preferences and limits. Another experience that affects sexual boundaries is the trauma from a difficult past. For example, someone who experienced sexual abuse would require boundaries to help them cope with triggers. Traumatic experiences should be treated and openly addressed with your partner. I know that it might be difficult to cope with the trauma, but if this is avoided or hidden, an unexpected trigger can cause intense harm.

Intellectual Boundaries

This kind of boundary allows us to be more open to the ideas and beliefs of other people. A good mindset allows us to practice understanding and respect. The world is filled with different people, and each of us is going through a series of emotions that we don't share entirely with the people close to us. I think that knowledge is brilliant, and we must constantly find ways to grow our minds, but some are often spoken down or slightly mocked. Be mindful of the other person's beliefs and thoughts, especially their curiosity.

Chapter 8:

Managing Boundary Violations

You can measure your worth by your dedication to your path, not by your successes or failures. –Elizabeth Gilbert

Boundary violations are common hurdles that each of us faces. According to Psych Central, most of us aren't aware that our boundaries have been crossed due to various forms of toxic relationships. Below are seven signs that your boundaries may have been crossed or violated (Casabianca, 2022, para. 1). Here are also some questions to consider when dealing with repeat boundary violations:

1. Who is this person violating your boundaries, and why do they have so much power over you?

2. Is this person (boundary violator) willing to change?

3. How long has this been going on?

4. Is the boundary violator aggressive or physically abusive?

5. How clear and consistent are your boundaries?

Signs That Your Boundaries Were Crossed

1. Codependent behaviors: Codependency is considered a disorder and is regarded as a dysfunctional relationship that allows one person to submissively follow the other.

This sort of relationship affects one's interpersonal skills, self-esteem, and self-worth. This is a severe disease that is known to worsen with symptoms over time and if left untreated.

- Characteristics of codependency: If you're in a codependent relationship, you likely have trouble expressing your feelings and setting boundaries. Also, you may find yourself in a toxic relationship with someone who is needy, dependent, or battling an addiction issue. Here are five characteristics to look out for:

  o Caretaking: You're often defined as a great caretaker with great empathetic skills, always willing to help someone through difficulty and trauma. The downside of this is that it is easy to be taken advantage of if you've been feeling depleted or emotionally drained after a conversation with someone. Or realize that you've endured burnout and feelings of resentment more regularly; this is a sign that you're losing control of your life.

  o Denial and avoidance: You're often denying and dismissing your own emotions and needs for the sake of the other person, and this is due to constantly having to care for the other person's needs. If you have trouble with confrontation and conflict, it may be a sign of codependency—avoiding your feelings and the actuality of the relationship. Also, if you feel that it's okay to dismiss your emotions for the sake of the other person because they're not as severe or serious, this is another sign of codependency.

- o Anger: Built-up anger leads to resentment, and this occurs when you suppress your own needs. If you're feeling voiceless or unseen in the relationship, it's a sign of imbalance in the relationship. The side effect of suppressing your emotions for the sake of the other person will lead to mental health problems for you.

- o Controlling: In the relationship, a lack of control is formed by the other person. If you find that your actions and emotions are constantly controlled by the other person's emotions and actions, it's a sign of unhealthy communication and codependency.

- o Enabling or rescuing: A more dangerous effect of the relationship is when toxic behaviors are encouraged, especially when violence and addiction tendencies are dismissed.

- Boundaries: Remember that the goal is to put yourself first. Because codependency is a toxic relationship, it's best to reach out for healthy forms of support. Here are some additional tips:

- o Improve your self-esteem (see chapter 2).

o Strengthen your communication skills (see chapter 3).

o Focus on your personal growth (see chapter 6).

2. Re-establishing the same boundary: This stems from someone blatantly ignoring and disregarding your boundaries despite the countless times you've shared the necessity of establishing them. Likely, this person won't stop ignoring your boundaries, and the next step would be to simply remove this person or induce some healthy space between the two of you.

- Boundaries: Most of the time, we find that our boundaries are too vague or not firm enough. If you don't express yourself confidently, it will affect the seriousness of the boundary or even its necessity. Here's what to do:

  o Create a consequence for the boundary being disrespected; let the person know that constant disrespect will jeopardize the relationship. However, remember that this isn't an ultimatum or a threat.

  o Limit your engagement with the person. Most people cross your boundaries because they want to garner a reaction from you; they want to see you fail.

  o Be consistent, don't reduce your morals, and respect yourself.

  o Stay calm and reflect after each incident.

3. Expressing discomfort: This form of violation stems from having to constantly express discomfort and being

ignored by the other person. You'll specifically recognize this issue if, after you've expressed discomfort, the person continues to disrespect your boundaries. If you find yourself constantly using the words "no," "stop it," or "I don't like that," these are clear signs that you need space to contemplate the relationship; this isn't healthy.

- Boundaries: Remember that you can't control someone else's reaction, so sticking around won't salvage the relationship if the other person isn't willing to change. Here are some tips to help you express your feelings:

  o Work on your communication skills (see chapter 3).

  o Be mindful of your body language (see chapter 3).

  o Re-establish your boundaries (see chapter 1).

4. Feeling off: This results from feeling physically sick every time your boundaries are crossed. The constancy has led you to feel sick and anxious; your palms might be sweaty or uncomfortable around certain individuals. These symptoms are normal bodily reactions whenever someone feels threatened.

- Boundaries: This sort of relationship will negatively impact your mental health; you may notice a rise in your anxiety levels or develop panic attacks; a rise in depression and paranoia; and may even develop post-traumatic stress disorder (PTSD).

5. You feel unacknowledged: This is due to your communication skills. A thing to remember is that communication goes both ways, so even if you're communicating effectively, if the other person isn't willing to reciprocate healthy communication, you won't make much progress.

   - Boundaries: The easiest thing to do for the relationship is to have an open and direct conversation with the person and strategize through pressure points in the relationship.

6. You feel mocked: Making jokes or teasing are toxic traits used to undermine the seriousness of your boundaries; it's also a form of manipulation people use to purposely cross lines. This is a clear sign that you're being violated and disrespected. If during confrontation you're being dismissed or gaslighted, it may be time to take a break from the relationship.

   - Boundaries: No one should be dismissing the seriousness of your boundaries; if they're treating it as a joke, they shouldn't be in your life until they are ready to respect you.

7. You feel pressured: This occurs when those around you constantly prohibit and dismiss the urgency or seriousness of your boundaries. You may feel as if they're constantly trying to undermine your boundaries or dismiss your emotions by calling you selfish.

   - Boundaries: These sorts of relationships will constantly make you aware of the issue or the negative influence on the relationship. Being made to feel this isn't healthy, and you shouldn't have to put up with this behavior.

How to Deal with People Who Violate Your Boundaries

1. Always reinforce your boundaries: It's normal for someone to come up against your boundaries and test them. We can't control what other people do; the only thing we're able to do is breathe and strengthen our boundaries. We previously discussed the removal of certain individuals—those who are constantly testing your boundaries despite how often you've expressed the need for the boundary—who are being toxic.

2. Reflect: We know that journaling is a great tool to use, and by taking the time to jot down our feelings, we are able to critically view our faults. Reflecting is going to help you adjust the boundary where necessary.

3. Respect yourself: Your boundaries shouldn't constantly be tested by someone you've expressed them to; in fact, if someone close to you is testing your boundaries, have a proper chat with them and let them know how you feel. Toxic relationships have a way of concealing their true motives; don't make excuses.

4. Accept that some people aren't meant to stay in your life: If it's time to move on from the relationship, do so. Try to have a chat with your friend, and if neither of you can agree on a suitable method of improvement, suggest a break from the relationship.

5. Breathe and detach: Try not to respond the same way as before whenever your boundaries are violated; don't engage with negativity. Instead, take a breath, acknowledge what was said or done, and walk away.

Again, it may be time to consider the necessity of the relationship.

How to Respect Other People's Boundaries

Here's additional information to keep in mind:

1. Take the time to understand the needs of the other person; this will help you comprehend their boundaries.

2. Watch out for non-verbal behavioral cues from the other person; this will let you know if the other person is uncomfortable. Remember that expressing boundaries is difficult and miscommunication is a common error, so commit to fully understanding what's happening.

3. Always be empathetic. It's difficult to know what the other person is experiencing emotionally; most of the time, we suppress our emotions so as not to draw attention to them.

4. Be receptive; this means that if you unknowingly crossed a boundary and were told so, don't question the boundary or the person. In fact, this is not the time to get upset or defensive; acknowledge it. If you require any information related to the boundary (so not to cross it again), do so kindly.

5. Understand that we each experience things differently and that you may be fine or comfortable with an issue, but the other person may not be. So, be mindful of your reactions and expectations.

6. Acknowledge the boundary being set; a great technique is to listen, reflect, and restate the boundary back to the person to make sure that you understand correctly.

7. Always apologize for crossing someone's boundaries; even if it was an accident, be respectful.

8. Forgive yourself for making mistakes; not every violation should be a massive insult or issue.

9. It's okay to ask for help; boundaries are complicated, and if you feel that you're constantly breaking someone's boundaries, reach out for help.

Be a Leader

More correctly, be the leader of yourself. Remember that the establishment of your boundaries is constructed by you. So, the sustainability of the boundary is reliant on your relationship with yourself, and yes, people can affect the health of the boundary negatively, but they are not in control of fully dismantling the boundary. As long as you're in a good place, you'll be fine, and so will your boundaries. Remember that the prioritization of goals is extremely important. Being the leader in your own life means that you're taking charge and controlling every positive and negative experience. Indeed, self-leadership is defined as being able to lead and achieve personal and professional success throughout your life. It's about being able to have an open and honest relationship with yourself about your goals, emotions, and overall behavior as a person (Indeed Editorial Team, 2022, para. 1). Here are some tips to help you improve your self-leadership skills:

1. Be comfortable with yourself: This means that you take the time to get to know yourself and what your purpose in life is. We discussed the benefits of self-awareness and mindfulness throughout this book. These skills, when paired with healthy boundaries, will positively affect your life and, ultimately, its future. Take the time to work on yourself.

2. Always take care of yourself: The great thing about prioritizing health with boundaries is that it's going to help you realize where you've been slacking. Mental health is extremely detrimental to your overall success in life, so be mindful of the people and experiences you find yourself in. We discussed the effects of change in our lives and how it tends to result in the loss of people. However, proper mental health care will prohibit stress, illness, burnout, and mental breakdowns.

3. Organize yourself: Make sure your goals are established and that your choices are clear and direct. Boundaries aim to prohibit stress, breakdowns, and ultimately feeling overwhelmed.

4. Always aim to be your best self: Constant practice will help you accomplish this task. When we live intentionally and use prioritization as a tool, we are generally more satisfied and at peace with ourselves.

5. Be patient: Don't rush the process. Trust and patience will ultimately help you achieve your goals and prepare you for the future.

Boundaries are lifelong entities that we carry with us into the future. Remember that momentary lapses won't define you or your capability to succeed. Always be intentional about your actions and choices and know that negativity can dissipate with a healthy and positive mindset. Trust yourself, and the process will simplify.

Conclusion

After all, tomorrow is another day! –Margaret Mitchell

I began this book because I couldn't cope with feeling overwhelmed by my surroundings. I've always been that person who could and would eventually resolve whatever was happening. I didn't think that this would run out or that I might lose my ability to press on and figure things out. I suppose the thing about getting older and finding perspective is true; this is exactly what happened to me. Instilling boundaries into my life changed so much for me. I know that uncomfortable change is often used to express the necessity of imposing change on your life. But it's true. I know that no one likes to be uncomfortable; honestly, I never did either. However, the belief that life exists without these challenging constructs is an old belief and attitude. Believe me, change can only improve your life, no matter how difficult it is.

However, I agree with the quotation above; tomorrow is another day, and I feel that the logic of this gets forgotten because we become too aware of failure and mistakes. Or we treat the presence of failure and mistakes as an intense hurdle to overcome. These days, if there's a flaw in my routine, I assure myself that tomorrow is another chance to get it right. I didn't entirely believe that the insertion of boundaries would result in a positive outcome in my life. Doubt factored into everything I did for such a long time, so if you finally reached the end of this book (thanks for sticking it out) and are doubtful about whether or not these practices are for you or worth your time, it's okay—I don't judge you. In fact, I'm going to encourage your doubt because it means you're being logical and also thinking about your own needs. Boundaries might seem cruel and imposing on the outside of things, but they're not; or at least that's not their intention. Though, I suppose one could argue that it is—aren't they supposed to stand tall against everything else that aims to cross them?

Anyway, I do think that boundaries are meant to instill might toward anyone they come in contact with, but this isn't to say that our boundaries should be feared. If there's anything we've learned along the way, it is that the first person the boundary comes into effect against is ourselves. We began this journey by learning about change and habits, and a common misinterpretation about habits is that they should be eviscerated. But we know that this is not true; eviscerating bad habits isn't logical, and to save you the trouble, evisceration holds no authority. Instead, we must approach our bad habits with a practical mindset and simply aim to switch them into healthier habits. Remember, this is possible; switching a bad thing into a good thing is recommended.

We learned that change naturally upsets the environment and those surrounding us; this is a normal response, and though it's discomforting, we must mind ourselves. A great step is to simply take a step back and let things and emotions unfold. Our next part of this journey was discovering what and how self-care practices worked. We learned that self-care is considered a skill that each individual must develop, and the great thing about skills is that they can be upskilled. A self-care practice is aimed at contributing to overall balance and well-being in our lives. The great thing about the self-care practice is its individuality. This means that because each of us is inherently different from the next person, the characteristics and attributes that design our personality determine what pillars of self-care will ultimately work for us.

We learned about intentional thinking and mindfulness, which basically means the same thing; this skill helps modulate our preferences and, most importantly, our values. There's no point in constructing a self-care practice if it doesn't work at bettering who you are. I shared an example of my practice and broke each of the pillars down into several chapters. Remember that there isn't a precise limit to how many pillars you can have and that it's okay for your concept of self-care not to match mine. In fact, you should never aim to mimic another person's idea of self-care. This is harmful to your overall health. Another thing that can be harmful is society itself. I know that we've touched on this narrative quite a bit.

It's frightening how much of our daily lives are informed by the opinions and guidance of society, isn't it? Listen, I'm not suggesting that you cut out social media (I mean, you can if you want to) or that you move to a secluded area where society cannot influence your mindset. I referred to boundaries as barriers that protect our values. When our boundaries are fed their nutrients, our mindsets are astounding devices. I mean, when our immune system is boosted with good health, so are our minds; each pillar, regardless of how many you have, is integrated into the next. So, doing well in one area naturally means that we'll do well in the next area.

But life is difficult, and sometimes we forget to be kind to ourselves. Again, this is why we have boundaries; they aim to look after us even when we cannot. I hope that the stories and information I shared with you thus far were enough to warrant trust and, if needed, a push toward pursuing healthy boundaries. I've come a long way since the establishment of my boundaries, and I confess that it's still difficult to establish them with people who don't feel or comprehend the need for these boundaries. Looking back on my boundaries, I think the ones I found most difficult were the relationship ones. At the beginning, I believed it would be simple to keep people out of my life. But it wasn't; the people that I believed would comprehend the most were the ones who didn't.

I might not have emphasized this a lot, but stamina is needed. Both physical and emotional stamina are needed to enforce your boundaries. There were moments when I considered enforcing only certain boundaries and disregarding others that appeared to be an issue for those around me. Trying to please people or trying to avoid confrontation will always be an issue for me. Don't get me wrong—I do my best to work on this daily. I have steps, and I do my best to stick to them. Remember, if you're setting a schedule, stick to it! However, dividing myself and my boundaries this way only affected my mental health. I remember feeling so guilty, and yet I couldn't name the reason for my guilt. My point is, always try to trust yourself and look toward the future. No matter how hard your difficulties are, I assure you that the hard work will pay off.

Looking back at the stories I've shared with you, I feel comforted knowing that you will find success across each pillar of your self-care practice. Boundaries are incredible devices, and sometimes I randomly overhear conversations between strangers wondering why neither of these people felt the need to browse the internet for more legitimate advice—it might be that their mindsets are fixed. However, here we are; the end feels odd, and I have an intense longing to continue writing. Before we reach that end, though, I want to bring up joy again. Remember that it's fed with self-care and that it's always present within us, regardless of what we're going through. Sometimes there are days when my mental health feels more negative or overly present within me.

It used to take a while for me to remember, but these days I simply breathe and remember that through joy I was able to craft meaningful relationships, and these relationships are my support systems. It's easy for me to message a friend and know that, if not immediately (people have responsibilities), a response will find its way to me. Joy has helped me be more mindful of myself; sometimes I'm able to break down a negative thought instantly—affirmations are good to have nearby. But mindfulness helps me reflect. Yesterday, anxiety lodged within me, and I left the room and asked myself, "Why are you anxious? What made you feel anxious? Where is it coming from?" I'm more compassionate with myself now. The point is, with care, we can all become better versions of ourselves.

Keep in mind that each of us has routines and boundaries to respect. I wish you all the best on your journey and welcome you back to this book if you need comfort and assurance.

If this book has resonated with you and fueled your determination to live authentically, I encourage you to share your thoughts in a short review. Your feedback will not only guide others towards this transformative resource but will also inspire me to continue empowering individuals like you on their boundary setting journey.

Remember as you navigate the art of setting boundaries, you are taking vital steps towards living a life of purpose, balance, and joy. Embrace each moment, cherish your progress, and know that you are capable of creating the fulfilling life you deserve.

Wishing you boundless success and happiness on your journey ahead, as you continue to master the art of setting boundaries with courage and self-compassion.

Thank you.

Eden Storm

References

Aakash. (n.d.) *What is psychological change? – everything you need to know.* MantraCare. https://mantracare.org/therapy/what-is/psychological-change/

Boyne, J., & Jeffers, O. (2013). *The terrible thing that happened to Barnaby Brocket.* Corgi.

Bray, L. (2007). *The sweet far thing.* Delacorte Press.

Casabianca, S.S. (2022, October 28). *7 signs someone doesn't respect your boundaries and what to do).* PsychCentral. https://psychcentral.com/relationships/signs-boundary-violations

Coelho, P., & Clarke, A. (2014). *The alchemist.* HarperOne.

Cuncic, A. (2022, November 9). *What is active listening?* Verywell Mind. https://www.verywellmind.com/what-is-active-listening-3024343

Dickens, C. (2008). *David Copperfield.* Oxford University Press.

Gawande, A. (2014). *Being mortal.* Anchor Canada.

Gay, R. (2014). *Bad feminist.* HarperCollins USA.

Gilbert, E. (2016). *Big magic.* Penguin USA.

Harvard Health Publishing. (2016, November 9). *Trade bad habits for good ones.* Harvard Health Publishing.

https://www.health.havard.edu/staying-healthy/trade-bad-habits-for-good-ones

Indeed Editorial Team. (2022, July 22). *What is self-leadership? 9 steps to develop your potential.* Indeed Career Guide. https://www.indeed.com/career-advice/career-development/self-leadership

Kakuzo, O. (2020). *Book of tea.* Collector's Library.

Merriam Webster. (2024). *Boundary.* Merriam Webster. https://www.merriam-webster.com/dictionary/boundary

Mitchell, M. (2017). *Gone with the wind.* Pan Books.

Nilon, L. (2021). *Spirituality, evolution & awakened consciousness: Getting real about soul maturity and spiritual growth.* Insight & Awareness.

Perry. E (2022, September 14). *What is self-awareness and how to develop it.* BetterUp. https://www.betterup.com/blog/what-is-self-awareness

Printed in Great Britain
by Amazon